On the Manipulation of Money and Credit

Three Treatises on Trade-Cycle Theory

 LUDWIG VON MISES

Translated and with a Foreword by Bettina Bien Greaves
Edited by Percy L. Greaves, Jr.

LIBERTY FUND *Indianapolis*

This book is published by Liberty Fund, Inc., a foundation established
to encourage study of the ideal of a society of free and responsible
individuals.

𒂼𒄄

The cuneiform inscription that serves as our logo and as the design
motif for our endpapers is the earliest-known written appearance of the
word "freedom" (*amagi*), or "liberty." It is taken from a clay document
written about 2300 B.C. in the Sumerian city-state of Lagash.

© 1978 by Liberty Fund, Inc.

New foreword and index © 2011 by Liberty Fund, Inc.
All rights reserved

On the Manipulation of Money and Credit was originally published in
1978 by Free Market Books.

Front cover photograph of Ludwig von Mises used by permission of the
Ludwig von Mises Institute, Auburn, Alabama.
Frontispiece courtesy of Bettina Bien Greaves.

Printed in the United States of America

C   10   9   8   7   6   5   4   3   2   1
P   10   9   8   7   6   5   4   3   2   1

Library of Congress Cataloging-in-Publication Data
Von Mises, Ludwig, 1881–1973.
   On the manipulation of money and credit: three treatises on
   trade-cycle theory / Ludwig von Mises; translated and with a fore-
   word by Bettina Bien Greaves; edited by Percy L. Greaves, Jr.
      p.   cm.
   Includes bibliographical references and index.
   ISBN 978-0-86597-761-7 (hardcover: alk. paper)—
   ISBN 978-0-86597-762-4 (pbk.: alk. paper)
      1. Monetary policy.   2. Credit.   3. Business cycles.
   I. Greaves, Percy L.   II. Greaves, Bettina Bien.   III. Title.

HB3723 .V664 2011
332.4'6—dc22   2009024020

Liberty Fund, Inc.
8335 Allison Pointe Trail, Suite 300
Indianapolis, Indiana 46250-1684

CONTENTS

This book is a collection of papers written by Mises during the 1920s and 1930s on money and the boom/bust trade cycle, the field in which one finds perhaps Mises's greatest contribution to economics. The papers included in this volume were first published in English with other materials by Free Market Books in 1978 and were reprinted later by the Ludwig von Mises Institute under the title *The Causes of Economic Crisis and Other Essays Before and After the Great Depression* (2006). Although Mises had long been interested in all aspects of monetary theory, these particular essays are devoted more specifically to his theory of monetary crises than are his other more general works.

Soon after Mises had earned his doctorate from the University of Vienna, he determined to write a book on money. To do a thorough job, he thought he should start with direct exchange, but he didn't believe he would have time, as he saw war looming in Europe. Although he had completed the compulsory military service required of all young men in the Austria-Hungary of his day, he would be subject to recall if war came. So he didn't begin with direct exchange but with indirect (nonbarter) exchange, building on the subjective marginal utility theory of value developed by his Austrian predecessors Carl Menger and Eugen von Böhm-Bawerk. His explanation was in direct opposition to the then-popular "state theory of money," which defined money as whatever the government decreed to be money.

That book, titled in German *Theorie des Geldes und der Umlaufsmittel*, appeared in 1912.[1] Mises explained there that money was a market phenomenon, which developed out of barter as individuals traded with one another in the attempt to discover something they could use

---

1. *Die Theorie des Geldes und der Umlaufsmittel* (Munich and Leipzig: Duncker & Humblot, 1912), expanded in 1924, and translated into English and first published in 1934 as *The Theory of Money and Credit* (Indianapolis: Liberty Fund, 1981).

as a medium of exchange. After dealing with money, Mises discussed banking. In this 1912 book he first raised the possibility that the banks might lower interest rates below market rates by increasing their issue of fiduciary media. Mises even considered that a bank might increase the quantity of money so much that its purchasing power might go down to 1/100th of its previous value, or even less if the monetary increases were continued. In that case, he then posited its purchasing power might decline until businesses would avoid it altogether and find something else to use as a medium of exchange. His contemporaries dismissed and discounted this possibility.

Mises described how the inflation (monetary expansion) fostered by the banks would lead to widespread price increases and economic malinvestment; however, if and when the banks stopped inflating, businesses would crash, the economy would stagnate, and all prices of goods and services would be readjusted. Thus, in 1912 Mises laid the groundwork for explaining the causes of the economic crises which afflicted capitalistic economies periodically and how to prevent them. But the world paid little attention; Mises's book was practically ignored, even ridiculed.

Mises's work in economics was interrupted by World War I, when he was called back into military service and served on the Eastern front. After the war, however, he continued to write on money. During the 1920s and 1930s, he built on and expanded the general monetary theory first set forth in *The Theory of Money and Credit,* and subsequently elaborated upon it in his later major works on economics, the German-language *Nationalökonomie* (1940) and its English language version, *Human Action* (1949).[2] The several monographs included in this present collection, written between the two World Wars, are devoted specifically to the theory of the trade cycle and include some of Mises's most important contributions to monetary theory.

My economist and historian husband, Percy L. Greaves, Jr.—like me, a longtime student of Mises—selected the papers included in this anthology as Mises's most important papers on money which had not previously appeared in English. The 1978 edition and 2006 reprint included an epilogue with articles on monetary theory by my husband. The epilogue has been omitted from this Liberty Fund edition in order to focus solely on the ideas of Mises.

---

2. *Human Action: An Economic Treatise* (Indianapolis: Liberty Fund, 2007).

In reading these works, keep in mind that Mises used the term "liberal" in the classical sense to refer to a free society and the term "inflation" to mean an increase in the quantity of money and credit, rather than one of the inevitable consequences of that increase, higher prices.

Bettina Bien Greaves
May 2008

ᘓ Stabilization of the Monetary Unit— From the Viewpoint of Theory

Introduction

Attempts to stabilize the value of the monetary unit strongly influence the monetary policy of almost every nation today. They must not be confused with earlier endeavors to create a monetary unit whose exchange value would not be affected by changes from the money side. In those olden and happier times, the concern was with how to bring the quantity of money into balance with the demand, without changing the purchasing power of the monetary unit. Thus, attempts were made to develop a monetary system under which no changes would emerge from the side of money to alter the ratios between the generally used medium of exchange (money) and other economic goods. The economic consequences of the widely deplored changes in the value of money were to be completely avoided.

There is no point nowadays in discussing why this goal could not then, and in fact cannot, be attained. Today we are motivated by other concerns. We should be happy just to return again to the monetary situation we once enjoyed. If only we had the gold standard back again, its shortcomings would no longer disturb us; we would just have to make the best of the fact that even the value of gold undergoes certain fluctuations.

Today's monetary problem is a very different one. During and after the war [World War 1, 1914–1918], many countries put into circulation vast quantities of credit money, which were endowed with legal tender quality. In the course of events described by Gresham's Law, gold disappeared from monetary circulation in these countries. These countries now have paper money, the purchasing power of which is

[*Die geldtheoretische Seite des Stabilisierungsproblems* (Schriften des Vereins für Sozialpolitik. Vol. 164, Part 2. Munich and Leipzig: Duncker & Humblot, 1923). Mises presented the original manuscript of this essay to the publisher in January 1923, more than eight months before the final breakdown of the German mark, but its publication was delayed.—Ed.]

subject to sudden changes. The monetary economy is so highly developed today that the disadvantages of such a monetary system, with sudden changes brought about by the creation of vast quantities of credit money, cannot be tolerated for long. Thus the clamor to eliminate the deficiencies in the field of money has become universal. People have become convinced that the restoration of domestic peace within nations and the revival of international economic relations are impossible without a sound monetary system.

I

The Outcome of Inflation

1.   Monetary Depreciation

If the practice persists of covering government deficits with the issue of notes, then the day will come without fail, sooner or later, when the monetary systems of those nations pursuing this course will break down completely. The purchasing power of the monetary unit will decline more and more, until finally it disappears completely. To be sure, one could conceive of the possibility that the process of monetary depreciation could go on forever. The purchasing power of the monetary unit could become increasingly smaller without ever disappearing entirely. Prices would then rise more and more. It would still continue to be possible to exchange notes for commodities. Finally, the situation would reach such a state that people would be operating with billions and trillions and then even higher sums for small transactions. The monetary system would still continue to function. However, this prospect scarcely resembles reality.

In the long run, trade is not helped by a monetary unit which continually deteriorates in value. Such a monetary unit cannot be used as a "standard of deferred payments." Another intermediary must be found for all transactions in which money and goods or services are not exchanged simultaneously. Nor is a monetary unit which continually depreciates in value serviceable for cash transactions either. Everyone becomes anxious to keep his cash holding, on which he continually suffers losses, as low as possible. All incoming money will be quickly spent. When purchases are made merely to get rid of money, which is shrinking in value, by exchanging it for goods of more enduring worth, higher prices will be paid than are otherwise indicated by other current market relationships.

In recent months, the German Reich has provided a rough picture of what must happen, once the people come to believe that the course of monetary depreciation is not going to be halted. If people are buying unnecessary commodities, or at least commodities not needed at the moment, because they do not want to hold on to their paper notes, then the process which forces the notes out of use as a generally acceptable medium of exchange has already begun. This is the beginning of the "demonetization" of the notes. The panicky quality inherent in the operation must speed up the process. It may be possible to calm the excited masses once, twice, perhaps even three or four times. However, matters must finally come to an end. Then there is no going back. Once the depreciation makes such rapid strides that sellers are fearful of suffering heavy losses, even if they buy again with the greatest possible speed, there is no longer any chance of rescuing the currency.

In every country in which inflation has proceeded at a rapid pace, it has been discovered that the depreciation of the money has eventually proceeded faster than the increase in its quantity. If m represents the actual number of monetary units on hand before the inflation began in a country, P represents the value then of the monetary unit in gold, M the actual number of monetary units which existed at a particular point in time during the inflation, and p the gold value of the monetary unit at that particular moment, then (as has been borne out many times by simple statistical studies):

$$mP > Mp.$$

On the basis of this formula, some have tried to conclude that the devaluation had proceeded too rapidly and that the actual rate of exchange was not justified. From this, others have concluded that the monetary depreciation is not caused by the increase in the quantity of money, and that obviously the Quantity Theory could not be correct. Still others, accepting the primitive version of the Quantity Theory, have argued that a further increase in the quantity of money was permissible, even necessary. The increase in the quantity of money should continue, they maintain, until the total gold value of the quantity of money in the country was once more raised to the height at which it was before the inflation began. Thus:

$$Mp = mP.$$

The error in all this is not difficult to recognize. For the moment, let us disregard the fact—which will be analyzed more fully below—that at the start of the inflation the rate of exchange on the Bourse,[1] as well as the agio [premium] against metals, races ahead of the purchasing power of the monetary unit expressed in commodity prices. Thus, it is not the gold value of the monetary units, but their temporarily higher purchasing power vis-à-vis commodities which should be considered. Such a calculation, with P and p referring to the monetary unit's purchasing power in commodities rather than to its value in gold, would also lead, as a rule, to this result:

$$mP > Mp.$$

However, as the monetary depreciation progresses, it is evident that the demand for money, that is for the monetary units already in existence, begins to decline. If the loss a person suffers becomes greater the longer he holds on to money, he will try to keep his cash holding as low as possible. The desire of every individual for cash no longer remains as strong as it was before the start of the inflation, even if his situation may not have otherwise changed. As a result, the demand for money throughout the entire economy, which can be nothing more than the sum of the demands for money on the part of all individuals in the economy, goes down.

To the extent to which trade gradually shifts to using foreign money and actual gold instead of domestic notes, individuals no longer invest in domestic notes but begin to put a part of their reserves in foreign money and gold. In examining the situation in Germany, it is of particular interest to note that the area in which Reichsmarks circulate is smaller today than in 1914,[2] and that now, because they have become poorer, the Germans have substantially less use for money. These circumstances, which reduce the demand for money, would exert much more influence if they were not counteracted by two factors which increase the demand for money:

1. The demand from abroad for paper marks, which continues to some extent today, among speculators in foreign exchange (Valuta); and

1. [*Bourse* (French). A continental European stock exchange, on which trades are also made in commodities and foreign exchange.—Ed.]
2. [The Treaty of Versailles at the end of World War I (1914–1918) reduced German-controlled territory considerably, restored Alsace-Lorraine to France, ceded large parts of West Prussia and Posen to Poland, ceded small areas to Belgium and stripped Germany of her former colonies in Africa and Asia.—Ed.]

2. The fact that the impairment of [credit] techniques for making payments, due to the general economic deterioration, may have increased the demand for money [cash holdings] above what it would have otherwise been.

2.   Undesired Consequences

If the future prospects for a money are considered poor, its value in speculations, which anticipate its future purchasing power, will be lower than the actual demand and supply situation at the moment would indicate. Prices will be asked and paid which more nearly correspond to anticipated future conditions than to the present demand for, and quantity of, money in circulation.

The frenzied purchases of customers who push and shove in the shops to get something, anything, race on ahead of this development; and so does the course of the panic on the Bourse where stock prices, which do not represent claims in fixed sums of money, and foreign exchange quotations are forced fitfully upward. The monetary units available at the moment are not sufficient to pay the prices which correspond to the anticipated future demand for, and quantity of, monetary units. So trade suffers from a shortage of notes. There are not enough monetary units [or notes] on hand to complete the business transactions agreed upon. The processes of the market, which bring total demand and supply into balance by shifting exchange ratios [prices], no longer function so as to bring about the exchange ratios which actually exist at the time between the available monetary units and other economic goods. This phenomenon could be clearly seen in Austria in the late fall of 1921.[3] The settling of business transactions suffered seriously from the shortage of notes.

Once conditions reach this stage, there is no possible way to avoid the undesired consequences. If the issue of notes is further increased, as many recommend, then things would only be made still worse.

3. [The post–World War I inflation in Austria is not as well known as the German inflation of 1923. The Austrian crown depreciated disastrously at that time, although not to the same extent as the German mark. The leader of the Christian-Social Party and chancellor of Austria (1922–1924 and 1926–1929), Dr. Ignaz Seipel (1876–1932), acting on the advice of Mises and some of his associates, succeeded in stopping the Austrian inflation in 1922.—Ed.]

Since the panic would keep on developing, the disproportionality between the depreciation of the monetary unit and the quantity in circulation would become still more exaggerated. The shortage of notes for the completion of transactions is a phenomenon of advanced inflation. It is the other side of the frenzied purchases and prices; it is the other side of the "crack-up boom."

3.   Effect on Interest Rates

Obviously, this shortage of monetary units should not be confused with what the businessman usually understands by a scarcity of money, accompanied by an increase in the interest rate for short-term investments. An inflation, whose end is not in sight, brings that about also. The old fallacy—long since refuted by David Hume and Adam Smith—to the effect that a scarcity of money, as defined in the businessman's terminology, may be alleviated by increasing the quantity of money in circulation, is still shared by many people. Thus, one continues to hear astonishment expressed at the fact that a scarcity of money prevails in spite of the uninterrupted increase in the number of notes in circulation. However, the interest rate is then rising, not in spite of, but precisely on account of, the inflation.

If a halt to the inflation is not anticipated, the money lender must take into consideration the fact that, when the borrower ultimately repays the sum of money borrowed, it will then represent less purchasing power than originally lent out. If the money lender had not granted credit but instead had used his money himself to buy commodities, stocks, or foreign exchange, he would have fared better. In that case, he would have either avoided loss altogether or suffered a lower loss. If he lends his money, it is the borrower who comes out well. If the borrower buys commodities with the borrowed money and sells them later, he has a surplus after repaying the borrowed sum. The credit transaction yields him a profit, a real profit, not an illusory, inflationary profit. Thus, it is easy to understand that, as long as the continuation of monetary depreciation is expected, the money lender demands, and the borrower is ready to pay, higher interest rates. Where trade or legal practices are antagonistic to an increase in the interest rate, the making of credit transactions is severely hampered. This explains the decline in savings among those groups of people for whom capital accumulation is possible only in the form of money deposits at banking institutions or through the purchase of securities at fixed interest rates.

4.   The Run from Money

The divorce of trade from a money that is proving increasingly useless begins with its being replaced from the hoards. If people want marketable goods available to meet unanticipated future needs, they start to accumulate other moneys—for instance, metallic (gold and silver) moneys, foreign notes, and occasionally also domestic notes which are valued more highly because their quantity cannot be increased by the government, such as the Romanov ruble of Russia or the "blue" money of Communist Hungary.[4] Then too, for the same purpose, people begin to acquire metal bars, precious stones and pearls, even pictures, other art objects and postage stamps. An additional step in displacing a no-longer-useful money is the shift to making credit transactions in foreign currencies or metallic commodity money which, for all practical purposes, means only gold. Finally, if the use of domestic money comes to a halt even in commodity transactions, wages too must be paid in some other way than with pieces of paper with which transactions are no longer being made.

Only the hopelessly confirmed statist can cherish the hope that a money, continually declining in value, may be maintained in use as money over the long run. That the German mark is still used as money today [January 1923] is due simply to the fact that the belief generally prevails that its progressive depreciation will soon stop, or perhaps even that its value per unit will once more improve. The moment that this opinion is recognized as untenable, the process of ousting paper notes from their position as money will begin. If the process can still be delayed somewhat, it can only denote another sudden shift of opinion as to the state of the mark's future value. The phenomena described as frenzied purchases have given us some advance warning as to how the process will begin. It may be that we shall see it run its full course.

Obviously the notes cannot be forced out of their position as the

4. [Moneys issued by no longer existing governments. The Romanovs were thrown out of power in Russia by the Communist Revolution in 1917; Hungary's post–World War I Communist government lasted only from March 21 to August 1, 1919.—Ed.]

legal media of exchange, except by an act of law. Even if they become completely worthless, even if nothing at all could be purchased for a billion marks, obligations payable in marks could still be legally satisfied by the delivery of mark notes. This means simply that creditors, to whom marks are owed, are precisely those who will be hurt most by the collapse of the paper standard. As a result, it will become impossible to save the purchasing power of the mark from destruction.

5.   Effect of Speculation

Speculators actually provide the strongest support for the position of the notes as money. Yet, the current statist explanation maintains exactly the opposite. According to this doctrine, the unfavorable configuration of the quotation for German money since 1914 is attributed primarily, or at least in large part, to the destructive effect of speculation in anticipation of its decline in value. In fact, conditions were such that during the war, and later, considerable quantities of marks were absorbed abroad precisely because a future rally of the mark's exchange rate was expected. If these sums had not been attracted abroad, they would necessarily have led to an even steeper rise in prices on the domestic market. It is apparent everywhere, or at least it was until recently, that even residents within the country anticipated a further reduction of prices. One hears again and again, or used to hear, that everything is so expensive now that all purchases, except those which cannot possibly be postponed, should be put off until later. Then again, on the other hand, it is said that the state of prices at the moment is especially favorable for selling. However, it cannot be disputed that this point of view is already on the verge of undergoing an abrupt change.

Placing obstacles in the way of foreign exchange speculation, and making transactions in foreign exchange futures especially difficult, were detrimental to the formation of the exchange rate for notes. Still, not even speculative activity can help at the time when the opinion becomes general that no hope remains for stopping the progressive depreciation of the money. Then, even the optimists will retreat from German marks and Austrian crowns, part company with those who anticipate a rise and join with those who expect a decline. Once only one view prevails on the market, there can be no more exchanges based on differences of opinion.

6.   Final Phases

The process of driving notes out of service as money can take place either relatively slowly or abruptly in a panic, perhaps in days or even hours. If the change takes place slowly that means trade is shifting, step by step, to the general use of another medium of exchange in place of the notes. This practice of making and settling domestic transactions in foreign money or in gold, which has already reached substantial proportions in many branches of business, is being increasingly adopted. As a result, to the extent that individuals shift more and more of their cash holdings from German marks to foreign money, still more foreign exchange enters the country. As a result of the growing demand for foreign money, various kinds of foreign exchange, equivalent to a part of the value of the goods shipped abroad, are imported instead of commodities. Gradually, there is accumulated within the country a supply of foreign moneys. This substantially softens the effects of the final breakdown of the domestic paper standard. Then, if foreign exchange is demanded even in small transactions, if, as a result, even wages must be paid in foreign exchange, at first in part and then in full, if finally even the government recognizes that it must do the same when levying taxes and paying its officials, then the sums of foreign money needed for these purposes are, for the most part, already available within the country. The situation, which emerges then from the collapse of the government's currency, does not necessitate barter, the cumbersome direct exchange of commodities against commodities. Foreign money from various sources then performs the service of money, even if somewhat unsatisfactorily.

Not only do incontrovertible theoretical considerations lead to this hypothesis. So does the experience of history with currency breakdowns. With reference to the collapse of the "Continental Currency" in the rebellious American colonies (1781), Horace White says: "As soon as paper was dead, hard money sprang to life, and was abundant for all purposes. Much had been hoarded and much more had been brought in by the French and English armies and navies. It was so plentiful that foreign exchange fell to a discount."[5]

In 1796, the value of French territorial mandats fell to zero. Louis Adolphe Thiers commented on the situation as follows:

---

5. White, Horace. *Money and Banking: Illustrated by American History.* Boston, 1895, p. 142. [*Op. cit.,* 5th ed., 1911, p. 99.—Ed.]

Nobody traded except for metallic money. The specie, which people had believed hoarded or exported abroad, found its way back into circulation. That which had been hidden appeared. That which had left France returned. The southern provinces were full of piasters, which came from Spain, drawn across the border by the need for them. Gold and silver, like all commodities, go wherever demand calls them. An increased demand raises what is offered for them to the point that attracts a sufficient quantity to satisfy the need. People were still being swindled by being paid in mandats, because the laws, giving legal tender value to paper money, permitted people to use it for the satisfaction of written obligations. But few dared to do this and all new agreements were made in metallic money. In all markets, one saw only gold or silver. The workers were also paid in this manner. One would have said there was no longer any paper in France. The mandats were then found only in the hands of speculators, who received them from the government and resold them to the buyers of national lands. In this way, the financial crisis, although still existing for the state, had almost ended for private persons.[6]

7.   Greater Importance of Money to a Modern Economy

Of course, one must be careful not to draw a parallel between the effects of the catastrophe, toward which our money is racing headlong on a collision course, with the consequences of the two events described above. In 1781, the United States was a predominantly agricultural country. In 1796, France was also at a much lower stage in the economic development of the division of labor and use of money and, thus, in cash and credit transactions. In an industrial country, such as Germany, the consequences of a monetary collapse must be entirely different from those in lands where a large part of the population remains submerged in primitive economic conditions.

6. Thiers, Louis Adolphe. *Histoire de la Révolution Française*. 7th ed., Vol. V. Brussels, 1838, p. 171. The interpretation placed on these events by the "School" of G. F. Knapp is especially fantastic. See H. Illig's *Das Geldwesen Frankreichs zur Zeit der ersten Revolution bis zum Ende der Papiergeldwährung* [*The French Monetary System at the Time of the First Revolution to the End of the Paper Currency*], Strassburg, 1914, p. 56. After mentioning attempts by the state to "manipulate the exchange rate of silver," he points out: "Attempts to reintroduce the desired cash situation began to succeed in 1796." Thus, even the collapse of the paper money standard was a "success" for the State Theory of Money. [Mises refers to *State Theory of Money* by Georg Friedrich Knapp (3rd German ed., 1921; English translation by H. M. Lucas and J. Bonar, London, 1924), which Mises credits with having popularized the idea that money is whatever the government decrees to be money.—Ed.]

Things will necessarily be much worse if the breakdown of the paper money does not take place step by step, but comes, as now seems likely, all of a sudden in panic. The supplies within the country of gold and silver money and of foreign notes are insignificant. The practice, pursued so eagerly during the war, of concentrating domestic stocks of gold in the central banks and the restrictions, for many years placed on trade in foreign moneys, have operated so that the total supplies of hoarded good money have long been insufficient to permit a smooth development of monetary circulation during the early days and weeks after the collapse of the paper note standard. Some time must elapse before the amount of foreign money needed in domestic trade is obtained by the sale of stocks and commodities, by raising credit, and by withdrawing balances from abroad. In the meantime, people will have to make out with various kinds of emergency money tokens.

Precisely at the moment when all savers and pensioners are most severely affected by the complete depreciation of the notes, and when the government's entire financial and economic policy must undergo a radical transformation, as a result of being denied access to the printing press, technical difficulties will emerge in conducting trade and making payments. It will become immediately obvious that these difficulties must seriously aggravate the unrest of the people. Still, there is no point in describing the specific details of such a catastrophe. They should only be referred to in order to show that inflation is not a policy that can be carried on forever. The printing presses must be shut down in time, because a dreadful catastrophe awaits if their operations go on to the end. No one can say how far we still are from such a finish.

It is immaterial whether the continuation of inflation is considered desirable or merely not harmful. It is immaterial whether inflation is looked on as an evil, although perhaps a lesser evil in view of other possibilities. Inflation can be pursued only so long as the public still does not believe it will continue. Once the people generally realize that the inflation will be continued on and on and that the value of the monetary unit will decline more and more, then the fate of the money is sealed. Only the belief, that the inflation will come to a stop, maintains the value of the notes.

II

The Emancipation of Monetary Value from the Influence of Government

1.   Stop Presses and Credit Expansion

The first condition of any monetary reform is to halt the printing presses. Germany must refrain from financing government deficits by issuing notes, directly or indirectly. The Reichsbank [Germany's central bank from 1875 until shortly after World War II] must not further expand its notes in circulation. Reichsbank deposits should be opened and increased, only upon the transfer of already existing Reichsbank accounts, or in exchange for payment in notes, or other domestic or foreign money. The Reichsbank should grant credits only to the extent that funds are available—from its own reserves and from other resources put at its disposal by creditors. It should not create credit to increase the amount of its notes, not covered by gold or foreign money, or to raise the sum of its outstanding liabilities. Should it release any gold or foreign money from its reserves, then it must reduce to that same extent the circulation of its notes or the use of its obligations in transfers.[1]

Absolutely no evasions of these conditions should be tolerated. However, it might be possible to permit a limited increase—for two or three weeks at a time—only to facilitate clearings at the end of quarters, especially at the close of September and December. This additional circulation credit introduced into the economy, above the otherwise strictly-adhered-to limits, should be statistically moderate and generally precisely prescribed by law.

1. Foreign currencies and similar legal claims could possibly be classed as foreign money. However, foreign money here obviously means only the money of countries with at least fairly sound monetary conditions.

There can be no doubt but that this would bring the continuing depreciation of the monetary unit to an immediate and effective halt. An increase in the purchasing power of the German monetary unit would even appear then—to the extent that the previous purchasing power of the German monetary unit, relative to that of commodities and foreign exchange, already reflected the view that the inflation would continue. This increase in purchasing power would rise to the point which corresponded to the actual situation.

2.   Relationship of Monetary Unit to World Money—Gold

However, stopping the inflation by no means signifies stabilization of the value of the German monetary unit in terms of foreign money. Once strict limits are placed on any further inflation, the quantity of German money will no longer be changing. Still, with changes in the demand for money, changes will also be taking place in the exchange ratios between German and foreign moneys. The German economy will no longer have to endure the disadvantages that come from inflation and continual monetary depreciation; but it will still have to face the consequences of the fact that foreign exchange rates remain subject to continual, even if not severe, fluctuations.

If, with the suspension of printing press operations, the monetary policy reforms are declared at an end, then obviously the value of the German monetary unit in relation to the world money, gold, would rise, slowly but steadily. For the supply of gold, used as money, grows steadily due to the output of mines while the quantity of the German money [not backed by gold or foreign money] would be limited once and for all. Thus, it should be considered quite likely that the repercussions of changes in the relationship between the quantity of, and demand for, money in Germany and in gold standard countries would cause the German monetary unit to rise on the foreign exchange market. An illustration of this is furnished by the developments of the Austrian money on the foreign exchange market in the years 1888–1891.

To stabilize the relative value of the monetary unit beyond a nation's borders, it is not enough simply to free the formation of monetary value from the influence of government. An effort should also be made to establish a connection between the world money and the German monetary unit, firmly binding the value of the Reichsmark to the value of gold.

It should be emphasized again and again that stabilization of the gold value of a monetary unit can only be attained if the printing presses are silenced. Every attempt to accomplish this by other means is futile. It is useless to interfere on the foreign exchange market. If the German government acquires dollars, perhaps through a loan, and sells the loan for paper marks, it is exerting pressure, in the process, on the dollar exchange rate. However, if the printing presses continue to run, the monetary depreciation will only be slowed down, not brought to a standstill as a result. Once the impetus of the intervention is exhausted, then the depreciation resumes again, even more rapidly. However, if the increase in notes has actually stopped, no intervention is needed to stabilize the mark in terms of gold.

3.   Trend of Depreciation

In this connection, it is pointed out that the increase in notes and the depreciation of the monetary unit do not exactly coincide chronologically. The value of the monetary unit often remains almost stable for weeks and even months, while the supply of notes increases continually. Then again, commodity prices and foreign exchange quotations climb sharply upward, in spite of the fact that the current increase in notes is not proceeding any faster or may even be slowing down. The explanation for this lies in the processes of market operations. The tendency to exaggerate every change is inherent in speculation. Should the conduct inaugurated by the few, who rely on their own independent judgment, be exaggerated and carried too far by those who follow their lead, then a reaction, or at least a standstill, must take place. So ignorance of the principles underlying the formation of monetary value leads to a reaction on the market.

In the course of speculation in stocks and securities, the speculator has developed the procedure which is his tool in trade. What he learned there he now tries to apply in the field of foreign exchange speculations. His experience has been that stocks which have dropped sharply on the market usually offer favorable investment opportunities and so he believes the situation to be similar with respect to the monetary unit. He looks on the monetary unit as if it were a share of stock in the government. When the German mark was quoted in Zurich at ten francs, one banker said: "Now is the time to buy marks. The German economy is surely poorer today than before the war so that a lower evaluation for the mark is justified. Yet the wealth of the German people has certainly not fallen to a twelfth of their prewar assets. Thus, the mark must rise in value." And when the Polish mark had fallen to five francs in Zurich, another banker said: "To me this low price is incomprehensible! Poland is a rich country. It has a profitable agricultural economy, forests, coal, petroleum. So the rate of exchange *should* be considerably higher."

Similarly, in the spring of 1919, a leading official of the Hungarian Soviet Republic[2] told me: "Actually, the paper money issued by the Hungarian Soviet Republic should have the highest rate of exchange, except for that of Russia. Next to the Russian government, the Hungarian government, by socializing private property throughout Hungary, has become the richest and thus the most credit-worthy in the world."

These observers do not understand that the valuation of a monetary unit depends *not* on the wealth of a country, but rather on the relationship between the quantity of, and demand for, money. Thus, even the richest country can have a bad currency and the poorest country a good one. Nevertheless, even though the theory of these bankers is false, and must eventually lead to losses for all who use it as a guide for action, it can temporarily slow down and even put a stop to the decline in the foreign exchange value of the monetary unit.

2. In power from March 21 to August 1, 1919, only.

The Return to Gold

1.   Eminence of Gold

In the years preceding and during the war, the authors who prepared the way for the present monetary chaos were eager to sever the connection between the monetary standard and gold. So, in place of a standard based directly on gold, it was proposed to develop a standard which would promise no more than a constant exchange ratio in foreign money. These proposals, insofar as they aimed at transferring control over the formulation of monetary value to government, need not be discussed any further. The reason for using a *commodity* money is precisely to prevent political influence from affecting directly the value of the monetary unit. Gold is not the standard money solely on account of its brilliance or its physical and chemical characteristics. Gold is the standard money primarily because an increase or decrease in the available quantity is independent of the orders issued by political authorities. The distinctive feature of the gold standard is that it makes changes in the quantity of money dependent on the profitability of gold production.

Instead of the gold standard, a monetary standard based on a foreign currency could be introduced. The value of the mark would then be related, *not* to gold, but to the value of a specific foreign money, at a definite exchange ratio. The Reichsbank would be ready at all times to buy or sell marks, in unlimited quantities at a fixed exchange rate, against the specified foreign money. If the monetary unit chosen as the basis for such a system is not on a sound gold standard, the conditions created would be absolutely untenable. The purchasing power of the German money would then hinge on fluctuations in the purchasing power of that foreign money. German policy would have renounced its influence on the creation of monetary value for the benefit of the policy of a foreign government. Then too, even if the foreign money, chosen as the basis for the German monetary unit, were on an absolutely sound gold standard at the moment, the possibility would remain that its tie to gold might be cut at some later time. So there is no basis for choosing this roundabout route in order to attain a sound monetary system. It is not true that adopting the gold standard leads to economic dependence on England, gold producers, or some other power. Quite the contrary! As a matter of fact, it is the monetary standard which relies on the money of a foreign government that deserves the name of a "subsidiary [dependent] or vassal standard."[1]

2.   Sufficiency of Available Gold

There are no grounds for saying that there is not enough gold available to enable all the countries in the world to have the gold standard. There can never be too much, nor too little, gold to serve the purpose of money. Supply and demand are brought into balance by the formation of prices. Nor is there reason to fear that prices generally would be depressed too severely by a return to the gold standard on the part of countries with depreciated currencies. The world's gold supplies have not decreased since 1914. They have increased. In view of the decline in trade and the increase in poverty, the demand for gold should be lower than it was before 1914, even after a complete return to the gold standard. After all, a return to the gold standard would not mean a return to the actual use of gold money within the country to pay for small- and medium-sized transactions. For even the gold exchange standard [Goldkernwährung] developed by Ricardo in his work, *Proposals for an Economical and Secure Currency* (1816), is a legitimate and adequate gold standard,[2] as the history of money in recent decades clearly shows.

Basing the German monetary system on some foreign money instead of the metal gold would have only one significance: By obscuring the true nature of reform, it would make a reversal easier for inflationist writers and politicians.

1. Schaefer, Carl A. *Klassische Valutastabilisierungen.* Hamburg, 1922, p. 65.
2. [By 1928, Mises had rejected the flexible (gold exchange) standard as adequate for curbing inflation and recommended a pure gold coin standard. See Mises's 1928 treatise, below, pp. 62–67.—Ed.]

The first condition of any real monetary reform is still to rout completely all populist doctrines advocating Chartism,[3] the creation of money, the dethronement of gold and free money. Any imperfection and lack of clarity here is prejudicial. Inflationists of every variety must be completely demolished. We should not be satisfied to settle for compromises with them. The slogan, "Down with gold," must be ousted. The solution rests on substituting in its place: "No governmental interference with the value of the monetary unit!"

3. [Chartism, an English working class movement, arose as a revolt against the Poor Law of 1834 which forced those able to work to enter workhouses before receiving public support. The movement was endorsed by both Marx and Engels and accepted the labor theory of value. Its members included those seeking inconvertible paper money and all sorts of political interventions and welfare measures. The advocates of various schemes were unified only in the advocacy of a charter providing for universal adult male suffrage, which each faction thought would lead to the adoption of its particular nostrums. Chartists' attempts to obtain popular support failed conspicuously and after 1848 the movement faded away.—Ed.]

The Money Relation

1. Victory and Inflation

No one can any longer maintain seriously that the rate of exchange for the German paper mark could be reestablished [in 1923] at its old gold value—as specified by the legislation of December 4, 1871, and by the coinage law of July 9, 1873. Yet many still resist the proposal to stabilize the gold value of the mark at the currently low rate. Rather vague considerations of national pride are often marshalled against it. Deluded by false ideas as to the causes of monetary depreciation, people have been in the habit of looking on a country's currency as if it were the capital stock of the fatherland and of the government. People believe that a low exchange rate for the mark is a reflection of an unfavorable judgment as to the political and economic situation in Germany. They do not understand that monetary value is affected only by changes in the relation between the demand for, and quantity of, money and the prevailing opinion with respect to expected changes in that relationship, including those produced by governmental monetary policies.

During the course of the war, it was said that "the currency of the victor" would turn out to be the best. But war and defeat on the field of battle can only influence the formation of monetary value indirectly. It is generally expected that a victorious government will be able to stop the use of the printing press sooner. The victorious government will find it easier both to restrict its expenditures and to obtain credit. This same interpretation would also argue that the rate of exchange of the defeated country would become more favorable as the prospects for peace improved. The values of both the German mark and the Austrian crown rose in October 1918. It was thought that a halt to the inflation could be expected even in Germany and Austria, but obviously this expectation was not fulfilled.

History shows that the foreign exchange value of the "victor's money" may also be very low. Seldom has there been a more brilliant victory than that finally won by the American rebels under Washington's leadership over the British forces. Yet the American money did not benefit as a result. The more proudly the Star Spangled Banner was raised, the lower the exchange rate fell for the "Continentals," as the paper notes issued by the rebellious states were called. Then, just as the rebels' victory was finally won, these "Continentals" became completely worthless. A short time later, a similar situation arose in France. In spite of the victory achieved by the Revolutionists, the agio [premium] for the metal rose higher and higher until finally, in 1796, the value of the paper monetary unit went to zero. In each case, the victorious government pursued inflation to the end.

2.   Establishing Gold "Ratio"

It is completely wrong to look on "devaluation" as governmental bankruptcy. Stabilization of the present depressed monetary value, even if considered only with respect to its effect on the existing debts, is something very different from governmental bankruptcy. It is both more and, at the same time, less than governmental bankruptcy. It is *more* than governmental bankruptcy to the extent that it affects not only public debts, but also all private debts. It is *less* than governmental bankruptcy to the extent that it affects only the government's outstanding debts payable in paper money, while leaving undisturbed its obligations payable in hard money or foreign currency. Then too, monetary stabilization brings with it no change in the relationships among contracting parties, with respect to paper money debts already contracted without any assurance of an increase in the value of the money.

To compensate the owners of claims to marks for the losses suffered, between 1914 and 1923, calls for something other than raising the mark's exchange rate. Debts originating during this period would have to be converted by law into obligations payable in old gold marks according to the mark's value at the time each obligation was contracted. It is extremely doubtful if the desired goal could be attained even by this means. The present title-holders to claims are not always the same ones who have borne the loss. The bulk of claims outstanding are represented by securities payable to the bearer and a considerable portion of all other claims have changed hands in the course of the years. When it comes to determining the currency profits and losses over the years, accounting methods are presented with tremendous obstacles by the technology of trade and the legal structure of business.

The effects of changes in general economic conditions on commerce, especially those of every cash-induced change in monetary value, and every increase in its purchasing power, militate against trying to raise the value of the monetary unit before [redefining and] stabilizing it in terms of gold. The value of the monetary unit should be [legally defined and] stabilized in terms of gold at the rate (ratio) which prevails at the moment.

As long as monetary depreciation is still going on, it is obviously impossible to speak of a specific "rate" for the value of money. For changes in the value of the monetary unit do not affect all goods and services throughout the whole economy at the same time and to the same extent. These changes in monetary value necessarily work themselves out irregularly and step by step. It is generally recognized that in the short or even the longer run, a discrepancy may exist between the value of the monetary unit, as expressed in the quotation for various foreign currencies, and its purchasing power in goods and services on the domestic market.

The quotations on the Bourse for foreign exchange always reflect speculative rates in the light of the currently evolving, but not yet consummated, change in the purchasing power of the monetary unit. However, the monetary depreciation, at an early stage of its gradual evolution, has already had its full impact on foreign exchange rates before it is fully expressed in the prices of all domestic goods and services. This lag in commodity prices, behind the rise of the foreign exchange rates, is of limited duration. In the last analysis, the foreign exchange rates are determined by nothing more than the anticipated future purchasing power attributed to a unit of each currency. The foreign exchange rates must be established at such heights that the purchasing power of the monetary unit remains the same, whether it is used to buy commodities directly, or whether it is first used to acquire another currency with which to buy the commodities. In the long run the rate cannot deviate from the ratio determined by its purchasing power. This ratio is known as the "natural" or "static" rate.

In order to stabilize the value of a monetary unit at its present value, the decline in monetary value must first be brought to a stop. The

value of the monetary unit in terms of gold must first attain some stability. Only then can the relationship of the monetary unit to gold be
given any lasting status. First of all, as pointed out above, the progress
of inflation must be blocked by halting any further increase in the issue of notes. Then one must wait awhile until after foreign exchange
quotations and commodity prices, which will fluctuate for a time,
have become adjusted. As has already been explained, this adjustment
would come about not only through an increase in commodity prices
but also, to some extent, with a drop in the foreign exchange rate.

Comments on the "Balance of Payments" Doctrine

1.   Refined Quantity Theory of Money

The generally accepted doctrine maintains that the establishment of sound relationships among currencies is possible only with a "favorable balance of payments." According to this view, a country with an "unfavorable balance of payments" cannot maintain the stability of its monetary value. In this case, the deterioration in the rate of exchange is considered structural and it is thought it may be effectively counteracted only by eliminating the structural defects.

The answer to this and to similar arguments is inherent in the Quantity Theory and in Gresham's Law.[1]

The Quantity Theory demonstrated that in a country which uses only commodity money, the "purely metallic currency" standard of the Currency Theory, money can never flow abroad continuously for any length of time. The outflow of a part of the gold supply brings about a contraction in the quantity of money available in the domestic market. This reduces commodity prices, promotes exports and restricts imports, until the quantity of money in the domestic economy is replenished from abroad. The precious metals being used as money are dispersed among the various individual enterprises and thus among the several national economies, according to the extent and intensity of their respective demands for money. Governmental interventions,

---

1. [Gresham's Law is often stated simply as "bad money drives out good." More precisely, this means that when the government has declared a depreciated money (bad money), the good commodity money (gold or silver) which has been legally undervalued vanishes from circulation, is sent abroad, and/or is hoarded. —Ed.]

which seek to regulate international monetary movements in order to assure the economy a "needed" quantity of money, are superfluous.

The undesirable outflow of money must always be simply the result of a governmental intervention which has endowed differently valued moneys with the same legal purchasing power. All that the government need do to avoid disrupting the monetary situation, and all it can do, is to abandon such interventions. That is the essence of the monetary theory of Classical economics and of those who followed in its footsteps, the theoreticians of the Currency School.[2]

With the help of modern subjective theory, this theory can be more thoroughly developed and refined. Still it cannot be demolished. And no other theory can be put in its place. Those who can ignore this theory only demonstrate that they are not economists.

2.   Purchasing Power Parity

One frequently hears, when commodity money is being replaced in one country by credit or token money—because the legally-decreed equality between the over-issued paper and the metallic money has prompted the sequence of events described by Gresham's Law—that it is the balance of payments that determines the rates of foreign exchange. That is completely wrong. Exchange rates are determined by the relative purchasing power per unit of each kind of money. As pointed out above, exchange rates must eventually be established at a height at which it makes no difference whether one uses a piece of money directly to buy a commodity, or whether one first exchanges this money for units of a foreign currency and then spends that foreign currency for the desired commodity. Should the rate deviate from that determined by the purchasing power parity, which is known as the "natural" or "static" rate, an opportunity would emerge for undertaking profit-making ventures.

It would then be profitable to buy commodities with the money which is legally *under*valued on the exchange, as compared with its purchasing power parity, and to sell those commodities for that money

2. [See *The Theory of Money and Credit* (Yale, 1953), pp. 180–86; (Liberty Fund, 1981), pp. 207–213.—Ed.]

which is legally *over*valued on the exchange, as compared with its actual purchasing power. Whenever such opportunities for profit exist, buyers would appear on the foreign exchange market with a demand for the undervalued money. This demand drives the exchange up until it reaches its "final rate."[3] Foreign exchange rates rise because the quantity of the [domestic] money has increased and commodity prices have risen. As has already been explained, it is only because of market technicalities that this cause and effect relationship is not revealed in the early course of events as well. Under the influence of speculation, the configuration of foreign exchange rates on the Bourse forecasts anticipated future changes in commodity prices.

The balance of payments doctrine overlooks the fact that the extent of foreign trade depends entirely on prices. It disregards the fact that nothing can be imported or exported if price differences, which make the trade profitable, do not exist. The balance of payments doctrine derives from superficialities. Anyone who simply looks at what is taking place on the Bourse every day and every hour sees, to be sure, only that the momentary state of the balance of payments is decisive for supply and demand on the foreign exchange market. Yet this diagnosis is merely the start of the inquiry into the factors determining foreign exchange rates. The next question is: What determines the momentary state of the balance of payments? This must lead only to the conclusion that the balance of payments is determined by the structure of prices and by the sales and purchases inspired by differences in prices.

3.　Foreign Exchange Rates

With rising foreign exchange quotations, foreign commodities can be imported only if they find buyers at their higher prices. One version of the balance of payments doctrine seeks to distinguish between the importation of necessities of life and articles which are considered less vital or necessary. It is thought that the necessities of life must be obtained at any price, because it is absolutely impossible to get along with-

---

3. See my paper "Zahlungsbilanz und Valutenkurse," *Mitteilungen des Verbandes österreichischer Banken und Bankiers*, II, 1919, pp. 39ff. [Pertinent paragraphs from this paper on the balance of payments fallacy have been translated and included below; see pp. 45–50.—Ed.]

out them. As a result, it is held that a country's foreign exchange must deteriorate continuously if it must import vitally-needed commodities while it can export only less-necessary items. This reasoning ignores the fact that the greater or lesser need for certain goods, the size and intensity of the demand for them, or the ability to get along without them is already fully expressed by the relative height of the prices assigned to the various goods on the market.

No matter how strong a desire the Austrians may have for foreign bread, meat, coal or sugar, they can satisfy this desire only if they can pay for them. If they want to import more, they must export more. If they cannot export more manufactured, or semi-manufactured, goods, they must export shares of stock, bonds, and titles to property of various kinds.

If the quantity of notes were not increased, then the prices of the items offered for sale would be lower. If they then demand more imported goods, the prices of these imported items must rise. Or else the rise in the prices of vital necessities must be offset by a decline in the prices of less vital articles, the purchase of which is restricted to permit the purchase of more necessities. Thus a general rise in prices is out of the question [without an increase in the quantity of notes]. The international payments would come into balance either with an increase in the export of dispensable goods or with the export of securities and similar items. It is only because the quantity of notes has been increased that they can maintain their imports at the higher exchange rates without increasing their exports. This is the only reason that the increase in the rate of exchange does not completely choke off imports and encourage exports until the "balance of payments" is once again "favorable."[4]

Certainly no proof is needed to demonstrate that speculation is not responsible for the deterioration of the foreign exchange situation. The foreign exchange speculator tries to anticipate prospective fluctuations in rates. He may perhaps blunder. In that case he must pay for his mistakes. However, speculators can never maintain for any length of time a quotation which is not in accord with market ratios. Governments and politicians, who blame the deterioration of the currency on speculation, know this very well. If they thought differently with respect

---

4. From the tremendous literature on the subject, I will mention here only T. E. Gregory's *Foreign Exchange Before, During and After the War*, London, 1921.

to future foreign exchange rates, they could speculate for the government's account, against a rise and in anticipation of a decline. By this single act they could not only improve the foreign exchange rate, but also reap a handsome profit for the Treasury.

4.   Foreign Exchange Regulations

The ancient Mercantilist fallacies paint a specter which we have no cause to fear. No people, not even the poorest, need abandon sound monetary policy. It is neither the poverty of the individual nor of the group, it is neither foreign indebtedness nor unfavorable conditions of production, that drives foreign exchange rates way up. Only inflation does this.

Consequently, every other means employed in the struggle against the rise in foreign exchange rates is useless. If the inflation continues, they will be ineffective. If there is no inflation, they are superfluous. The most significant of these other means is the prohibition or, at least, the restriction of the importation of certain goods which are considered dispensable, or at least not vitally necessary. The sums of money within the country which would have been spent for the purchase of these goods are now used for other purchases. Obviously, the only goods involved are those which would otherwise have been sold abroad. These goods are now bought by residents within the country at prices higher than those bid for them by foreigners. As a result, on the one side there is a decline in imports and thus in the demand for foreign exchange, while on the other side there is an equally large reduction in exports and thus also a decline in the supply of foreign exchange. Imports are paid for by exports, not with money as the superficial Neo-mercantilist doctrine still maintains.

If one really wants to check the demand for foreign exchange, then, to the extent that one wants to reduce imports, money must actually be taken away from the people—perhaps through taxes. This sum should be completely withdrawn from circulation, not even given out for government purposes, but rather destroyed. This means adopting a policy of deflation. Instead of restricting the importation of chocolate, wine and cigarettes, the sums people would have spent for these commodities must be taken away from them. The people would then either have to reduce their consumption of these or of some other commodities. In the former case [i.e., if the consumption of imported goods is reduced] less foreign exchange is sought. In the latter case [i.e., if the consumption of domestic articles declines] more goods are exported and thus more foreign exchange becomes available.

It is equally impossible to influence the foreign exchange market by prohibiting the hoarding of foreign moneys. If the people mistrust the reliability of the value of the notes, they will seek to invest a portion of their cash holdings in foreign money. If this is made impossible, then the people will either sell fewer commodities and stocks or they will buy more commodities, stocks, and the like. However, they will certainly not hold more domestic currency in place of foreign exchange. In any case, this behavior reduces total exports. The demand for foreign exchange for hoarding disappears and, at the same time, the supply of foreign exchange coming into the country in payment of exports declines. Incidentally, it may be mentioned that making it more difficult to amass foreign exchange hampers the accumulation of a reserve fund that could help the economy weather the critical time which immediately follows the collapse of a paper monetary standard. As a matter of fact, this policy could eventually lead to even more serious trouble.

It is entirely incomprehensible how the idea originates that making the export of one's own notes more difficult is an appropriate method for reducing the foreign exchange rate. If fewer notes leave the country, then more commodities must be exported or fewer imported. The quotation for notes on exchange markets abroad does not depend on the greater or lesser supplies of notes available there. Rather, it depends on commodity prices. The fact that foreign speculators buy up notes and hoard them, leading to a speculative boom, is only likely to raise their quoted price. If the sums held by foreign speculators had remained within the country, the domestic commodity prices and, as a result, the "final rate" of foreign exchange would have been driven up still higher.

If inflation continues, neither foreign exchange regulations nor control of foreign exchange clearings can stop the depreciation of the monetary unit abroad.

VI

The Inflationist Argument

1. Substitute for Taxes

Nowadays, the thesis is maintained that sound monetary relationships may certainly be worth striving for, but public policy is said to have other higher and more important goals. As serious an evil as inflation is, it is not considered the most serious. If it is a choice of protecting the homeland from enemies, feeding the starving and keeping the country from destruction, then let the currency go to rack and ruin. And if the German people must pay off a tremendous war debt, then the only way they can help themselves is through inflation.

This line of reasoning in favor of inflationism must be sharply distinguished from the old inflationist argument which actually approved of the economic consequences of continual monetary depreciation and considered inflationism a worthwhile political goal. According to the later doctrine, inflationism is still considered an evil although, under certain circumstances, a lesser evil. In its eyes, monetary depreciation is not considered the inevitable outcome of a certain pattern of economic conditions, as it is by adherents of the "balance of payments" doctrine discussed in the preceding section. Advocates of limited inflationism tacitly, if not openly, admit in their argumentation that paper money inflation, as well as the resulting monetary depreciation, is always a product of inflationist policy. However, they believe that a government may get into a situation in which it would be more advantageous to counter a greater evil with the lesser evil of inflationism.

The argument for limited inflationism is often stated so as to represent inflationism as a kind of a tax which is called for under certain conditions. In some situations it is considered more advantageous to cover government expenditures by issuing new notes, than by increasing the burden of taxes or borrowing money. This was the argument during the war, when it was a question of defraying the expenses of army and navy. The same argument is now advanced when it comes to supplying some of the population with cheap foodstuffs, covering the operating deficits of public enterprises (the railroads, etc.) and arranging for reparations payments. The truth is that inflationism is resorted to when raising taxes is considered disagreeable and when borrowing is considered impossible. The question now is to explore the reasons why it is considered disagreeable or impossible to employ these two normally routine ways of obtaining money for government expenditures.

2.   Financing Unpopular Expenditures

High taxes can be imposed only if the general public is in agreement with the purposes for which the funds collected will be used. In this connection, it is worth noting that the higher the general burden of taxes, the more difficult it becomes to deceive public opinion as to the fact that the taxes cannot be borne by the more affluent minority of the population alone. Even taxes levied on property owners and the more affluent affect the entire economy. Their indirect effects on the less well-to-do are often felt more intensely than would be those from direct proportional taxation. It may not be easy to detect these relationships when tax rates are relatively low, but they can hardly be overlooked when taxes are higher. However, there is no doubt that the present system of taxing "property" can hardly be carried any farther than it already has been in the countries where inflationism now prevails. Thus the decision will have to be made to rely more directly on the masses for providing funds. For policy makers who enjoy the confidence of the masses only if they impose no obvious sacrifice, this is something they dare not risk.

Can anyone doubt that the warring peoples of Europe would have tired of the conflict much sooner, if their governments had clearly, candidly, and promptly presented them with the bill for military expenses? No war party in any European country would have dared to levy any considerable taxes on the masses to pay the costs of the war. Even in England, the printing presses were set in motion. Inflation had the great advantage of creating an appearance of economic well-being, of an increase of wealth. It also concealed capital consumption by falsifying monetary calculations. The inflation led to illusory entrepreneurial and capitalistic profits, which could be taxed as income at especially high rates. This could be done without the masses, and frequently even without the taxpayers themselves, noticing that a portion of capital itself was being taxed away. Inflation made it possible to turn the anger of the people against "war profiteers, speculators and smugglers." Thus, inflation proved itself an excellent psychological aid to the pro-war policy, leading to destruction and annihilation.

What the war began, the revolution continues. A socialistic or semi-socialistic government needs money to operate unprofitable enterprises, to subsidize the unemployed and to provide the people with cheap food supplies. Yet, it cannot raise the funds through taxes. It dares not tell the people the truth. The pro-statist, pro-socialist doctrine calling for government operation of the railroads would lose its popularity very quickly if a special tax were levied to cover the operating losses of the government railroads. If the Austrian masses themselves had been asked to pay a special bread tax, they would very soon have realized from whence came the funds to make the bread cheaper.

3. War Reparations

The decisive factor for the German economy is obviously the payment of the reparations burden imposed by the Treaty of Versailles and its supplementary agreements. According to Karl Helfferich,[1] these payments imposed on the German people an annual obligation estimated at two-thirds of their national income. This figure is undoubtedly much too high. No doubt, other estimates, especially those pronounced by French observers, considerably underestimate the actual ratio. In any event, the fact remains that a very sizeable portion of Germany's current income is consumed by the levy imposed on the nation, and that, if the specified sum is to be withdrawn every year from income, the living standard of the German people must be substantially reduced.

Even though somewhat hampered by the remnants of feudalism, an authoritarian constitution and the rise of statism and socialism, capitalism was able to develop to a considerable extent on German soil. In recent generations, the capitalistic economic system has multiplied

1. Helfferich, Karl. *Die Politik der Erfüllung*. Munich, 1922, p. 22. [Helfferich (1872–1924), as minister of the German Imperial Treasury, 1915–1916, and later in various official and unofficial positions, helped pave the way for the 1923 inflation.—Ed.]

German wealth many times over. In 1914, the German economy could support three times as many people as a hundred years earlier and still offer them incomparably more. The war and its immediate consequences have drastically reduced the living standards of the German people. Socialistic destruction has continued this process of impoverishment. Even if the German people did not have to fulfill any reparations payments, they would still be much, much poorer than they were before the war. The burden of these obligations must inevitably reduce their living standard still further—to that of the thirties and forties of the last century. It may be hoped that this impoverishment will lead to a reexamination of the socialist ideology which dominates the German spirit today, that this will succeed in removing the obstacles now preventing an increase in productivity, and that the unlimited opening up of possibilities for development, which exist under capitalism and *only* under capitalism, will increase many times over the output of German labor. Still the fact remains that if the obligation assumed is to be paid for out of income, the only way is to produce more and consume less.

A part of the burden, or even all of it, could of course be paid off by the export of capital goods. Shares of stock, bonds,[2] business assets, land, buildings, would have to be transferred from German to foreign ownership. This would also reduce the total income of the people in the future, if not right away.

4.   The Alternatives

These various means, however, are the only ways by which the reparations obligations can be met. Goods or capital, which would otherwise have been consumed within the country, can be exported. To discuss which is more practical is not the task of this essay. The only question which concerns us is how the government can proceed in order to shift to the individual citizens the burden of payments, which devolves first of all on the German treasury. Three ways are possible: raising taxes; borrowing within the country; and issuing paper money. Whichever one of the three methods may be chosen, the nature of its effect abroad remains unaltered. These three ways differ only in their distribution of the burden among citizens.

2. Thus, raising a foreign loan falls within this category too.

If the funds are collected by raising a domestic loan, then subscribers to the loan must either reduce their consumption or dispose of a part of their capital. If taxes are imposed, then the taxpayers must do the same. The funds which flow from taxes or loans into the government treasury and which it uses to buy gold, foreign bills of exchange, and foreign currencies to fulfill its foreign liabilities are supplied by the lenders and the taxpayers through the sale abroad of commodities and capital goods. The government can only purchase available foreign exchange which comes into the country from these sales. So long as the government has the power to distribute only those funds which it receives from tax payments and the floating of loans, its purchases of foreign exchange cannot push up the price of gold and foreign currencies. At any one time, the government can buy only so much gold and foreign exchange as the citizens have acquired through export sales. In fact, the world prices of goods and services cannot rise on this account. Rather their prices will decline as a consequence of the larger quantities offered for sale.

However, if and as the government follows the third route, issuing new notes in order to buy gold and foreign exchange instead of raising taxes and floating loans, then its demand for gold and foreign exchange, which is obviously not counterbalanced by a proportionate supply, drives up the prices of various kinds of foreign money. It then becomes advantageous for foreigners to acquire more marks so as to buy capital goods and commodities within Germany at prices which do not yet reflect the new ratios. These purchases drive prices up in Germany right away and bring them once again into adjustment with the world market. This is the actual situation. The foreign exchange, with which reparations obligations are paid, comes from sales abroad of German capital and commodities. The only difference consists in how the government obtains the foreign exchange. In this case, the government first buys the foreign exchange abroad with marks, which the foreigners then use to make purchases in Germany, rather than the German government's acquiring the foreign exchange from those within Germany who have received payment for previous sales abroad.

From this one learns that the continuing depreciation of the German mark cannot be the consequence of reparations payments. The depreciation of the mark is simply a result of the fact that the government supplies the funds needed for the payments through new issues of notes. Even those who wish to attribute the decline in the rate of exchange on the market to the payment of reparations, rather than to inflation, point out that the quotation for marks is inevitably disturbed by the government's offering of marks for the purchase of foreign exchange.[3] Still, if the government had available for these foreign exchange purchases only the number of marks which it received from taxes or loans, then its demand would not exceed the supply. It is only because it is offering newly created notes that it drives the foreign exchange rates up.

5. The Government's Dilemma

Nevertheless, this is the only method available for the German government to defray the reparations debt. Should it try to raise the sums demanded through loans or taxes, it would fail. As conditions with the German people are now, if the economic consequences of compliance were clearly understood and there was no deception as to the costs of that policy, the government could not count on majority support for it. Public opinion would turn with tremendous force against any government that tried to carry out in full the obligations to the Allied Powers. It is not our task to explore whether or not that might be a wise policy.

However, saying that the decline of the value of the German mark is not the direct consequence of making reparations payments but is due rather to the methods the German government uses to collect the funds for the payments, by no means has the significance attached to it by the French and other foreign politicians. They maintain that it is justifiable, from the point of view of world policy, to burden the German people with this heavy load. This explanation of the German monetary depreciation has absolutely nothing to do with whether, in view of the terms of the Armistice, the Allied demand, in general, and its height, in particular, are founded on justice.

The only significant thing for us, however, since it explains the political role of the inflationist procedure, is yet another insight. We have seen that if a government is not in a position to negotiate loans and

---

3. See Walter Rathenau's addresses—January 12, 1922, before the Senate of the Allied Powers at Cannes, and March 29, 1922, to the Reichstag (Cannes und Genua, *Vier Reden zum Reparationsproblem*, Berlin, 1922, pp. 11ff. and 34ff.). [Rathenau (1867–1922), a German industrialist, became minister of reconstruction (1921) and foreign minister (1922) in the post–World War I German government.—Ed.]

does not dare levy additional taxation for fear that the financial and general economic effects will be revealed too clearly too soon, so that it will lose support for its program, it always considers it necessary to undertake inflationary measures. Thus inflation becomes one of the most important psychological aids to an economic policy which tries to camouflage its effects. In this sense, it may be described as a tool of anti-democratic policy. By deceiving public opinion, it permits a system of government to continue which would have no hope of receiving the approval of the people if conditions were frankly explained to them.

Inflationist policy is never the necessary consequence of a specific economic situation. It is always the product of human action—of man-made policy. For whatever the reason, the quantity of money in circulation is increased. It may be that the people are influenced by incorrect theoretical doctrines as to the way the value of money develops and are not aware of the consequences of this action. It may be that, in full knowledge of the effects of inflation, they are purposely aiming, for some reason, at a reduction in the value of the monetary unit. So no apology can ever be given for inflationist policy. If it rests on theoretically incorrect monetary doctrines, then it is inexcusable, for there should never, never be any forgiveness for wrong theories. If it rests on a definite judgment as to the effects of monetary depreciation, then to *want* to "excuse it" is inconsistent. If monetary depreciation has been knowingly engineered, its advocates would not want to excuse it but rather to try to demonstrate that it was a good policy. They would want to show that, under the circumstances, it was even better to depreciate the money than to raise taxes further or to permit the deficit-ridden, nationalized railroads to be transferred from government control to private hands.

Even governments must learn once more to adjust their outgo to income. Once the end results to which inflation must lead are recognized, the thesis that a government is justified in issuing notes to make up for its lack of funds will disappear from the handbooks of political strategy.

VII

The New Monetary System

1.   First Steps

The bedrock and cornerstone of the provisional new monetary system
must be the absolute prohibition of the issue of any additional notes not
completely covered by gold. The maximum limit for German notes in
circulation [not completely covered by gold] will be the sum of the banknotes, Loan Bureau Notes (Darlehenskassenscheinen), emergency currency (Notgeld) of every kind, and small coins, actually in circulation at
the instant of the monetary reform, less the gold stock and supply of foreign bills held in the reserves of the Reichsbank and the private banks of
issue. There must be absolutely no expansion above this maximum under any circumstances, except for the relaxation mentioned above at the
end of each quarter. [See pp. 15–16.] Notes of any kind over and above
this amount must be fully covered by deposits of gold or foreign exchange in the Reichsbank. As may be seen, this constitutes acceptance
of the leading principle of Peel's Bank Act, with all its shortcomings.
However, these flaws have little significance at the moment. Our first
concern is only to get rid of the inflation by stopping the printing presses.
This goal, the only immediate one, will be most effectively served by a
strict prohibition of the issue of additional notes not backed by metal.

Once adjustments have been made to the new situation, then it will
be time enough to consider:

1. On the one hand, whether it might not perhaps be expedient to
   tolerate the issue, within very narrow limits, of notes not covered
   by metal.
2. On the other hand, whether it might not also be necessary to limit
   similarly the issue of other fiduciary media by establishing regulations over the banks' cash balances and their check and draft
   transactions.

The question of banking freedom must then be discussed, again and again, on basic principles. Still, all this can wait until later. What is needed now is only to prohibit the issue of additional notes not covered by metal. This is all that can be done at present. Ideally, the limitation on the issue of currency could also be extended, even now, to the Reichsbank's transfer balances (deposits).[1] However, this is not of as critical importance, for the present currency inflation has been and can be brought about only by the issue of notes.

Simultaneously with the enactment of the prohibition against the issue of additional notes not covered by metal, the Reichsbank should be required to purchase all supplies of gold offered them in exchange for notes at prices precisely corresponding to the new ratio. At the same time, the Reichsbank should be obliged to supply any amount of gold requested at that ratio, to anyone able to offer German notes in payment. With this reform, the German standard would become a gold exchange standard (Goldkernwährung). Later will be time enough to examine whether or not to renounce permanently the actual circulation of gold within the country. Careful consideration should be given to whether or not the higher costs needed to maintain the actual circulation of gold within the country might not be amply repaid by the fact that this would permit the people to discontinue using notes. Weaning the people away from paper money could perhaps forestall future efforts aimed at the over-issue of notes endowed with legal tender status. Nevertheless, the gold exchange standard is undoubtedly sufficient for the time being.[2] The legal rate for notes in making payments can be temporarily maintained without risk.

It should also be specifically pointed out that the obligation of the Reichsbank to redeem its notes must be interpreted in the strictest possible manner. Every subterfuge, by which European central banks sought to follow some form of "gold premium policy"[3] during the decades preceding the World War, must be discontinued.

---

1. See p. 15 above.

2. [Mises later rejected this position. See below, pp. 62–67. See also *Human Action*, Chapter XXXI, Section 3, and his 1953 essay, "Monetary Reconstruction," the epilogue to *The Theory of Money and Credit*, 1953 and later editions.—Ed.]

3. [The "gold premium policy" made gold expensive by hampering its export, manipulating discount rates, and limiting the redemption of domestic money in gold.—Ed.]

2.   Market Interest Rates

If the Reichsbank were operating under these principles, it would obviously not be in a position to supply the money market with funds obtained by increasing the circulation of notes not covered by metal. Except for the possibilities of such transfers as may not have been previously limited, the Bank will be able to lend out only its own resources and funds furnished by its creditors. Inflationary increases in the note circulation for the benefit of private, as well as public, credit demands will thus be ruled out. The Bank will not then be in a position to follow the policy—which it has attempted again and again—of lowering artificially the market rate of interest.

The explanation of the balance of payments doctrine presented here shows that under this arrangement the Reichsbank would not run the risk of an outflow of its gold and foreign exchange (Devisen) holdings. Citizens lacking confidence in future banking policy, who in the early years of the new monetary system try to exchange notes for gold or foreign exchange (Devisen), will not be satisfied with the assertion that the Bank will be required to redeem its notes only in larger sums, for gold bars and foreign exchange, not for gold coins. Then it will not be possible to eliminate all notes from circulation. In the beginning a larger amount [of foreign currencies and metallic money] may even be withdrawn from the Bank and hoarded. However, as soon as some confidence in the reliability of the new money develops, the hoards of foreign moneys and gold accumulated will flow into the Bank.

The Reichsbank must renounce every attempt to lower interest rates below those which reflect the actual supply and demand relationships existing in the capital markets, and thus encourage the demand for loans which can only be made by increasing the quantity of notes. This prerequisite for monetary reform will evoke the criticism of the naive inflationists of the business world. These criticisms will grow as the difficulties of providing credit for the German economy increase during the coming years. In the view of the businessman, the role of the central bank of issue is to provide cheap credit. The businessman believes that the Bank should not deny newly created notes to those who want additional credit. For decades, the errors of the English Banking School theoreticians have prevailed in Germany. Bendixen has recently made them popular through his easily readable *Theorie der klassischen Geldschöpfung.*[4]

People keep forgetting that the increase in the cost of credit—which has become known by the very misleading term "scarcity of money"—cannot be overcome in the long run by inflationist measures. They also forget that the interest rate cannot be reduced in the long run by credit expansion. The expansion of credit always leads to higher commodity prices and quotations for foreign exchange and foreign moneys.

4. [Friedrich Bendixen (1864–1920); no English translations of his works are known.—Ed.]

VIII

The Ideological Meaning of Reform

1.   The Ideological Conflict

The purely materialistic doctrine now used to explain every event looks on monetary depreciation as a phenomenon brought about by certain "material" causes. Attempts are made to counteract these imagined causes by various monetary techniques. People ignore, perhaps knowingly, that the roots of monetary depreciation are ideological in nature. It is always an inflationist policy, not "economic conditions," which brings about the monetary depreciation. The evil is philosophical in character. The state of affairs, universally deplored today, was created by a misunderstanding of the nature of money and an incorrect judgment as to the consequences of monetary depreciation.

Inflationism, however, is not an isolated phenomenon. It is only one piece in the total framework of politico-economic and socio-philosophical ideas of our time. Just as the sound money policy of gold standard advocates went hand in hand with liberalism, free trade, capitalism and peace, so is inflationism part and parcel of imperialism, militarism, protectionism, statism and socialism. Just as the world catastrophe, which has swept over mankind since 1914, is not a natural phenomenon but the necessary outcome of the ideas which dominate our time, so also is the monetary crisis nothing but the inevitable consequence of the supremacy of certain ideologies concerning monetary policy.

Statist Theory has tried to explain every social phenomenon by the operation of mysterious power factors. It has disputed the possibility that economic laws for the formation of prices could be demonstrated. Failing to recognize the significance of commodity prices for the development of exchange relationships among various moneys, it has tried to distinguish between the domestic and foreign values of money.

It has tried to attribute changes in exchange rates to various causes—the balance of payments, speculative activity, and political factors. Ignoring completely the Currency Theory's important criticism of the Banking Theory, Statist Theory has actually prescribed the Banking Theory. It has moreover even revived the doctrine of the canonists and of the legal authorities of the Middle Ages to the effect that money is a creature of the government and the legal order. Thus, Statist Theory prepared the philosophical groundwork from which the inflationism of recent years developed.

The belief that a sound monetary system can once again be attained without making substantial changes in economic policy is a serious error. What is needed first and foremost is to renounce all inflationist fallacies. This renunciation cannot last, however, if it is not firmly grounded on a full and complete divorce of ideology from all imperialist, militarist, protectionist, statist, and socialist ideas.

Balance of Payments and Foreign Exchange Rates

The printing press played an important role in creating the means for carrying on the war. Every belligerent nation and many neutral ones used it. With the cessation of hostilities, however, no halt was called to the money-creating activities of the banks of issue. Previously, notes were printed to finance the war. Today, notes are still being printed, at least in some countries, to satisfy domestic demands of various kinds. The entire world is under the sway of inflation. The prices of all goods and services rise from day to day and no one can say when these increases will come to an end.

Inflation today is a general phenomenon, but its magnitude is not the same in every country. The increase in the quantity of money in the different currency areas is neither equal statistically—an equality which, given the different demands for money in the different areas, would be *apparent* only—nor has the increase proceeded in all areas in the same ratio to the demand for money. Thus, price increases, insofar as they are due to changes from the money side, have not been the same everywhere. . . .

Price increases, which are called into existence by an increase in the quantity of money, do not appear overnight. A certain amount of time passes before they appear. The additional quantity of money enters the economy at a certain point. It is only from there, step by step, that it is dispersed. It goes first to certain individuals in the economy only and to certain branches of production. As a result, in the beginning it raises the demand for certain goods and services only, not for all of them. Only later do the prices of other goods and services also rise. Foreign

[Excerpted from "Zahlungsbilanz und Devisenkurse" in *Mitteilungen des Verbandes Oesterreichischer Banken und Bankiers*, Vol. 2, #3–4, 1919.—Ed.]

exchange quotations, however, are speculative rates of exchange—that is, they arise out of the transactions of business people, who, in their operations, consider not only the present but also potential future developments. Thus, the depreciation of the money becomes apparent relatively soon in the foreign exchange quotations on the Bourse—long before the prices of other goods and services are affected. . . .

Now, there is one theory which seeks to explain the formation of foreign exchange rates by the balance of payments, rather than by a currency's purchasing power. This theory makes a distinction in the depreciation of the money between the decline in the currency's value on international markets and the reduction in its purchasing power domestically. It maintains that there is only a very slight connection between the two or, as many say, no connection at all. The exchange rate of foreign currencies is a result of the momentary balance of payments. If the payments going abroad rise without a corresponding increase in the payments coming into the country, or if the payments coming from abroad should decline without a corresponding reduction of the payments going out of the country, then foreign exchange rates must rise.

We shall not speculate on the reasons why such a theory can be advanced. Between the change in the exchange rates for foreign currencies and the change in the monetary unit's domestic purchasing power, there is usually a time lag—shorter or longer. Therefore, superficial observation could very easily lead to the conclusion that the two data were independent of one another. We have also heard that the balance of payments is the immediate cause of the daily fluctuations in exchange rates. A theory which explained surface appearances only and did not analyze the situation thoroughly could easily overlook the facts that (a) the day-to-day ratio between the supply of and demand for foreign exchange determined by the balance of payments can evoke only transitory variations from the "static" rate formed by the purchasing power of various kinds of money, (b) these deviations must disappear promptly, and (c) these variations will vanish more quickly and more completely the less restraints are imposed on trade and the freer speculation is.

Certainly there shouldn't be any reason to examine this theory further. It has been settled scientifically. The fact that it plays a significant role in economic policy may be a reason for investigating the political basis for its undoubted popularity among government officials and writers. Still that may be left to others.

However, we must concern ourselves with a new variety of this balance of payments doctrine which originated with the war. People say it may be generally true that the purchasing power of the money, rather than the balance of payments, determines the exchange rate of foreign currencies. But now, in view of the reduction of trade brought about by the war, this is not the case. Since trade is hampered, the process which would restore the disrupted "static" exchange ratios among foreign currencies is held in check. As a result, therefore, the balance of payments becomes decisive for the exchange rates of foreign currencies.[1] If it is desired to raise the foreign exchange rate, or to keep it from declining further, one must try to establish a favorable balance of payments. . . .

The basic fallacy in this theory is that it completely ignores the fact that the height of imports and exports depends primarily on prices. Neither imports nor exports are undertaken out of caprice or just for fun. They are undertaken to carry on a profitable trade, that is to earn money from the differences in prices on either side. Thus imports or exports are carried on until price differences disappear. . . .

The balance of payments doctrine of foreign exchange rates completely overlooks the meaning of prices for the international movement of goods. It proceeds erroneously from the act of payment, instead of from the business transaction itself. That is a result of the pseudo-legal monetary theory—a theory which has brought the most cruel consequences to German science—the theory which looks on money as a means of payment only, and not as a general medium of exchange.

When deciding to undertake a business transaction, a merchant does not ignore the costs of obtaining the necessary foreign currency until the time when the payment actually comes due. A merchant who proceeded in this way would not long remain a merchant. The merchant takes the ratio of foreign currency very much into account in his calculations, as he always has an eye to the selling price. Also, whether he hedges against future changes in the exchange rate, or whether he bears the risk himself of shifts in foreign currency values, he considers the anticipated fluctuations in foreign exchange. The same situation prevails *mutatis mutandis* with reference to tourist traffic and international freight. . . .

It is easy to recognize that we find here only a new form of the old

---

1. For the sake of completeness only, it should be mentioned that the adherents of this theory attribute domestic price increases not to the inflation, but to the shortage of goods exclusively.

favorable and unfavorable balance of trade theory championed by the Mercantilist School of the sixteenth to eighteenth centuries. That was before the widespread use of banknotes and other bank currency. The fear was then expressed that a country with an unfavorable balance of trade could lose its entire supply of the precious metals to other lands. Therefore, it was held that by encouraging exports and limiting imports so far as possible, a country could take precautions to prevent this from happening. Later, the idea developed that the trade balance alone was not decisive, that it was only *one* factor in creating the balance of payments and that the entire balance of payments must be considered. As a result, the theory underwent a partial reorganization. However, its basic tenet—namely that when a government did not control its foreign trade relations, all its precious metals might flow abroad—persisted until it lost out finally to the hard-hitting criticism of Classical economics.

The balance of payments of a country is nothing but the sum of the balances of payments of all its individual enterprises. The essence of every balance is that the debit and credit sides are equal. If one compares the credit entries and the debit entries of an enterprise the two totals must be in balance. The situation can be no different in the case of the balance of payments of an entire country. Then too, the totals must always be in balance. This equilibrium, that must necessarily prevail because goods are exchanged—not given away—in economic trading, is not brought about by undertaking all exports and imports first, without considering the means of payment, and then only later adjusting the balance in money. Rather, money occupies precisely the same position in undertaking a transaction as do the other commodities being exchanged. Money may even be the usual reason for making exchanges.

In a society in which commodity transactions are monetary transactions, every individual enterprise must always take care to have on hand a certain quantity of money. It must not permit its cash holding to fall below the definite sum considered necessary for carrying out its transactions. On the other hand, an enterprise will not permit its cash holding to exceed the necessary amount, for allowing that quantity of money to lie idle will lead to loss of interest. If it has too little money, it must reduce purchases or sell some wares. If it has too much money, then it must buy goods.

For our purposes here, it is immaterial whether the enterprise buys producers' or consumers' goods. In this way, every individual sees to it that he is not without money. Because everyone pursues his own interest in doing this, it is impossible for the free play of market forces to cause a drain of all money out of a city, a province or an entire country. The government need not concern itself with this problem any more than does the city of Vienna with the loss of its monetary stock to the surrounding countryside. Nor—assuming a precious metals standard (the purely metallic currency of the English Currency School)—need government concern itself with the possibility that the entire country's stock of precious metals will flow out.

If we had a pure gold standard, therefore, the government need not be in the least concerned about the balance of payments. It could safely relinquish to the market the responsibility for maintaining a sufficient quantity of gold within the country. Under the influence of free trade forces, precious metals would leave the country only if a surplus was on hand and they would always flow in if too little was available, in the same way that all other commodities are imported if in short supply and exported if in surplus. Thus, we see that gold is constantly moving from large-scale gold producing countries to those in which the demand for gold exceeds the quantity mined—without the need for any government action to bring this about.[2] . . .

It may be asked, however, doesn't history show many examples of countries whose metallic money (gold and silver) has flown abroad? Didn't gold coins disappear from the market in Germany just recently? Didn't the silver coins vanish here at home in Austria? Isn't this evidence a clear-cut contradiction of the assertion that trade spontaneously maintains the monetary stock? Isn't this proof that the state needs to interfere in the balance of payments?

However, these facts do not in the least contradict our statement. Money does not flow out because the balance of payments is unfavorable and because the state has not interfered. Rather, money flows out precisely because the state *has* intervened and the interventions have called forth the phenomenon described by the well-known Gresham's Law. The government itself has ruined the currency by the steps it has taken. And then the government tries in vain, by other measures, to restore the currency it has ruined.

2. See Hertzka, *Das Wesen des Geldes*, Leipzig, 1887, pp. 44ff.; Wieser, "Der Geldwert und seine Veränderungen" (*Schriften des Vereins für Sozialpolitik*, Vol. 132), Leipzig, 1910, pp. 530ff.

The disappearance of gold money from trade follows from the fact that the state equates, in terms of legal purchasing power, a lesser-valued money with a higher-valued money. If the government introduces into trade quantities of inconvertible banknotes or government notes, then this must lead to a monetary depreciation. The value of the monetary unit declines. However, this depreciation in value can affect only the inconvertible notes. Gold money retains all, or almost all, of its value internationally. However, since the state—with its power to use the force of law—declares the lower-valued monetary notes equal in purchasing power to the higher-valued gold money and forbids the gold money from being traded at a higher value than the paper notes, the gold coins must vanish from the market. They may disappear abroad. They may be melted down for use in domestic industry. Or they may be hoarded. That is the phenomenon of good money being driven out by bad, observed so long ago by Aristophanes, which we call Gresham's Law.

No special government intervention is needed to retain the precious metals in circulation within a country. It is enough for the state to renounce all attempts to relieve financial distress by resorting to the printing press. To uphold the currency, it need do no more than that. And it need do *only* that to accomplish this goal. All orders and prohibitions, all measures to limit foreign exchange transactions, etc., are completely useless and purposeless.

If we had a pure gold standard, measures to prevent a gold outflow from the country due to an unfavorable balance of payments would be completely superfluous. He who has no money to buy abroad, because he has neither exported goods nor performed services abroad, will be able to buy abroad only if foreigners give him credit. However, his foreign purchases then will in no way disturb the stability of the domestic currency. . . .

❧ Monetary Stabilization
and Cyclical Policy

Preface

In recent years the problems of monetary and banking policy have been approached more and more with a view to both stabilizing the value of the monetary unit and eliminating fluctuations in the economy. Thanks to serious attempts at explaining and publicizing these most difficult economic problems, they have become familiar to almost everyone. It may perhaps be appropriate to speak of fashions in economics, and it is undoubtedly the "fashion" today to establish institutions for the study of business trends.

This has certain advantages. Careful attention to these problems has eliminated some of the conflicting doctrines which had handicapped economics. There is only one theory of monetary value today—the Quantity Theory. There is also only one trade cycle theory—the Circulation Credit Theory, developed out of the Currency Theory and usually called the "Monetary Theory of the Trade Cycle." These theories, of course, are no longer what they were in the days of Ricardo and Lord Overstone. They have been revised and made consistent with modern subjective economics. Yet the basic principle remains the same. The underlying thesis has merely been elaborated upon. So despite all its defects, which are now recognized, due credit should be given the Currency School for its achievement.

In this connection, just as in all other aspects of economics, it becomes apparent that scientific development goes steadily forward. Every single step in the development of a doctrine is necessary. No intellectual effort applied to these problems is in vain. A continuous, unbroken line of scientific progress runs from the Classical authors down to the modern writers. The accomplishment of Gossen, Menger,

[*Geldwertstabilisierung und Konjunkturpolitik* (Jena: Gustav Fischer, 1928)—Ed.]

Walras and Jevons, in overcoming the apparent antinomy of value during the third quarter of the last century, permits us to divide the history
of economics into two large subdivisions—the Classical, and the Modern or Subjective. Still it should be remembered that the contributions
of the Classical School have not lost all value. They live on in modern
science and continue to be effective.

Whenever an economic problem is to be seriously considered, it is
necessary to expose the violent rejection of economics which is carried on everywhere for political reasons, especially on German soil.
Nothing concerning the problems involved in either the creation
of the purchasing power of money or economic fluctuations can be
learned from Historicism or Nominalism. Adherents of the Historical-
Empirical-Realistic School and of Institutionalism either say nothing at all about these problems, or else they depend on the very same
methodological and theoretical grounds which they otherwise oppose.
The Banking Theory, until very recently certainly the leading doctrine, at least in Germany, has been justifiably rejected. Hardly anyone
who wishes to be taken seriously dares to set forth the doctrine of the
elasticity of the circulation of fiduciary media—its principal thesis and
cornerstone.[1]

However, the popularity attained by the two political problems of
stabilization—the value of the monetary unit and fiduciary media—
also brings with it serious disadvantages. The popularization of a theory always contains a threat of distorting it, if not of actually demolish-
ing its very essence. Thus the results expected of measures proposed
for stabilizing the value of the monetary unit and eliminating business
fluctuations have been very much overrated. This danger, especially in
Germany, should not be underestimated. During the last ten years, the
systematic neglect of the problems of economic theory has meant that

---

1. Sixteen years ago when I presented the Circulation Credit Theory of the crisis in the first
German edition of my book on *The Theory of Money and Credit* (1912), I encountered ignorance
and stubborn rejection everywhere, especially in Germany. The reviewer for Schmoller's Yearbook [*Jahrbuch für Gesetzgebung, Verwaltung und Volkswirtschaft*] declared: "The conclusions
of the entire work [are] simply not discussable." The reviewer for Conrad's Yearbook [*Jahrbuch
für Nationalökonomie und Statistik*] stated: "Hypothetically, the author's arguments should not
be described as completely wrong; they are at least coherent." But his final judgment was "to
reject it anyhow." Anyone who follows current developments in economic literature closely,
however, knows that things have changed basically since then. The doctrine which was ridiculed once is widely accepted today.

no attention has been paid to accomplishments abroad. Nor has any benefit been derived from the experiences of other countries.

The fact is ignored that proposals for the creation of a monetary unit with "stable value" have already had a hundred year history. Also ignored is the fact that an attempt to eliminate economic crises was made more than eighty years ago—in England—through Peel's Bank Act (1844). It is not necessary to put all these proposals into practice to see their inherent difficulties. However, it is simply inexcusable that so little attention has been given during recent generations to the understanding gained, or which might have been gained if men had not been so blind, concerning monetary policy and fiduciary media.

Current proposals for a monetary unit of "stable value" and for a non-fluctuating economy are, without doubt, more refined than were the first attempts of this kind. They take into consideration many of the less important objections raised against earlier projects. However, the basic shortcomings, which are necessarily inherent in all such schemes, cannot be overcome. As a result, the high hopes for the proposed reforms must be frustrated.

If we are to clarify the possible significance—for economic science, public policy and individual action—of the cyclical studies and price statistics so widely and avidly pursued today, they must be thoroughly and critically analyzed. This can, by no means, be limited to considering cyclical changes only. "A theory of crises," as Böhm-Bawerk said, "can never be an inquiry into just one single phase of economic phenomena. If it is to be more than an amateurish absurdity, such an inquiry must be the last, or the next to last, chapter of a written or unwritten economic system. In other words, it is the final fruit of knowledge of all economic events and their interconnected relationships."[2]

Only on the basis of a comprehensive theory of indirect exchange, i.e., a theory of money and banking, can a trade cycle theory be erected. This is still frequently ignored. Cyclical theories are carelessly drawn up and cyclical policies are even more carelessly put into operation. Many a person believes himself competent to pass judgment, orally and in writing, on the problem of the formulation of monetary value and the rate of interest. If given the opportunity—as legislator or manager of a country's monetary and banking policy—he feels called

---

2. *Zeitschrift für Volkswirtschaft, Sozialpolitik und Verwaltung.* Vol. VII, p. 132.

upon to enact radical measures without having any clear idea of their consequences. Yet, nowhere is more foresight and caution necessary than precisely in this area of economic knowledge and policy. For the superficiality and carelessness with which social problems are wont to be handled soon misfire if applied in this field. Only by serious thought directed at understanding the interrelationship of all market phenomena can the problems we face here be satisfactorily solved.

Stabilization of the Purchasing Power of the Monetary Unit

The Problem

1.   "Stable Value" Money

Gold and silver had already served mankind for thousands of years as generally accepted media of exchange—that is, as money—before there was any clear idea of the formation of the exchange relationship between these metals and consumers' goods, i.e., before there was an understanding as to how money prices for goods and services are formed. At best, some attention was given to fluctuations in the mutual exchange relationships of the two precious metals. But so little understanding was achieved that men clung, without hesitation, to the naive belief that the precious metals were "stable in value" and hence a useful measure of the value of goods and prices. Only much later did the recognition come that supply and demand determine the exchange relationship between money, on the one hand, and consumers' goods and services, on the other. With this realization, the first versions of the Quantity Theory, still somewhat imperfect and vulnerable, were formulated. It was known that violent changes in the volume of production of the monetary metals led to all-round shifts in money prices. When "paper money" was used alongside "hard money," this connection was still easier to see. The consequences of a tremendous paper inflation could not be mistaken.

From this insight, the doctrine of monetary policy emerged that the issue of "paper money" should be avoided completely. However, before long other authors made still further stipulations. They called the attention of politicians and businessmen to the fluctuations in the purchasing power of the precious metals and proposed that the substance of monetary claims be made independent of these variations. Side by side with money as the standard of deferred payments,[1] or in place of it, there should be a tabular, index, or multiple commodity standard. Cash transactions, in which the terms of both sides of the contract are fulfilled simultaneously, would not be altered. However, a new procedure would be introduced for credit transactions. Such transactions would not be completed in the sum of money indicated in the contract. Instead, either by means of a universally compulsory legal regulation or else by specific agreement of the two parties concerned, they would be fulfilled by a sum with the purchasing power deemed to correspond to that of the original sum at the time the contract was made. The intent of this proposal was to prevent one party to a contract from being hurt to the other's advantage. These proposals were made more than one hundred years ago by Joseph Lowe (1822) and repeated shortly thereafter by G. Poulett Scrope (1833).[2] Since then, they have cropped up repeatedly but without any attempt having been made to put them into practice anywhere.

2.　　Recent Proposals

One of the proposals, for a multiple commodity standard, was intended simply to supplement the precious metals standard. Putting it into practice would have left metallic money as a universally acceptable medium of exchange for all transactions not involving deferred monetary payments. (For the sake of simplicity in the discussion that follows, when referring to metallic money we shall speak only of gold.) Side by side with gold as the universally acceptable medium of exchange, the index or multiple commodity standard would appear as a standard of deferred payments.

Proposals have been made in recent years, however, which go still farther. These would introduce a "tabular," or "multiple commodity," standard for *all* exchanges when one commodity is not exchanged directly for another. This is essentially Keynes' proposal. Keynes wants to oust gold from its position as money. He wants gold to be replaced

---

1. Standard of deferred payments is "Zahlungsmittel" in German. Unfortunately this German expression must be avoided today because, its meaning has been so compromised through its use by Nominalists and Chartists that it brings to mind the recently exploded errors of the "state theory of money."

2. Jevons, Wm. Stanley. *Money and the Mechanism of Exchange*, 13th ed. London, 1902, pp. 328ff.

by a paper standard, at least for trade within a country's borders. The government, or the authority entrusted by the government with the management of monetary policy, should regulate the quantity in circulation so that the purchasing power of the monetary unit would remain unchanged.[3]

The American, Irving Fisher, wants to create a standard under which the paper dollar in circulation would be redeemable, not in a previously specified weight of gold, but in a weight of gold which has the same purchasing power the dollar had at the moment of the transition to the new currency system. The dollar would then cease to represent a fixed amount of gold with changing purchasing power and would become a changing amount of gold supposedly with unchanging purchasing power. It was Fisher's idea that the amount of gold which would correspond to a dollar should be determined anew from month to month, according to variations detected by the index number.[4] Thus, in the view of both these reformers, in place of monetary gold, the value of which is independent of the influence of government, a standard should be adopted which the government "manipulates" in an attempt to hold the purchasing power of the monetary unit stable.

However, these proposals have not as yet been put into practice anywhere, although they have been given a great deal of careful consideration. Perhaps no other economic question is debated with so much ardor or so much spirit and ingenuity in the United States as that of stabilizing the purchasing power of the monetary unit. Members of the House of Representatives have dealt with the problem in detail. Many scientific works are concerned with it. Magazines and daily papers devote lengthy essays and articles to it, while important organizations seek to influence public opinion in favor of carrying out Fisher's ideas.

3. Keynes, John Maynard. A *Tract on Monetary Reform*. London, 1923; New York, 1924, pp. 177ff.
4. Fisher, Irving. *Stabilizing the Dollar*. New York, 1925, pp. 79ff.

II

The Gold Standard

1.   The Demand for Money

Under the gold standard, the formation of the value of the monetary unit is not *directly* subject to the action of the government. The production of gold is free and responds only to the opportunity for profit. All gold not introduced into trade for consumption or for some other purpose flows into the economy as money, either as coins in circulation or as bars or coins in bank reserves. Should the increase in the quantity of money exceed the increase in the demand for money, then the purchasing power of the monetary unit must fall. Likewise, if the increase in the quantity of money lags behind the increase in the demand for money, the purchasing power of the monetary unit will rise.[1]

There is no doubt about the fact that, in the last generation, the purchasing power of gold has declined. Yet earlier, during the two decades following the German monetary reform and the great economic crisis of 1873, there was widespread complaint over the decline of commodity prices. Governments consulted experts for advice on how to eliminate this generally prevailing "evil." Powerful political parties recommended measures for pushing prices up by increasing the quantity of money. In place of the gold standard, they advocated the silver standard, the double standard [bimetallism] or even a paper standard, for they considered the annual production of gold too small to meet the growing demand for money without increasing the purchasing power of the monetary unit. However, these complaints died out in the last five years of the nineteenth century, and soon men everywhere began to grumble about the opposite situation, i.e., the increasing cost

1. This is not the place to examine further the theory of the formation of the purchasing power of the monetary unit. In this connection, see *The Theory of Money and Credit* [(Yale, 1953) pp. 97–165 and (Liberty Fund, 1981), pp. 117–189.—Ed.].

of living. Just as they had proposed monetary reforms in the 1880's and 1890's to counteract the *drop* in prices, they *now* suggested measures to stop prices from rising.

The general advance of the prices of all goods and services in terms of gold is due to the state of gold production and the demand for gold, both for use as money as well as for other purposes. There is little to say about the production of gold and its influence on the ratio of the value of gold to that of other commodities. It is obvious that a smaller increase in the available quantity of gold might have counteracted the depreciation of gold. Nor need anything special be said about the industrial uses of gold. But the third factor involved, the way demand is created for gold as money, is quite another matter. Very careful attention should be devoted to this problem, especially as the customary analysis ignores most unfairly this monetary demand for gold.

During the period for which we are considering the development of the purchasing power of gold, various parts of the world, which formerly used silver or credit money ("paper money") domestically, have changed over to the gold standard. Everywhere, the volume of money transactions has increased considerably. The division of labor has made great progress. Economic self-sufficiency and barter have declined. Monetary exchanges now play a role in phases of economic life where earlier they were completely unknown. The result has been a decided increase in the demand for money. There is no point in asking whether this increase in the demand for cash holdings by individuals, together with the demand for gold for non-monetary uses, was sufficient to counteract the effect on prices of the new gold flowing into the market from production. Statistics on the height and fluctuations of cash holdings are not available. Even if they could be known, they would tell us little because the changes in prices do not correspond with changes in the relationship between supply and demand for cash holdings. Of greater importance, however, is the observation that the increase in the demand for money is not the same thing as an increase in the demand for gold for monetary purposes.

As far as the individual's cash holding is concerned, claims payable in money, which may be redeemed at any time and are universally considered safe, perform the service of money. These money substitutes—small coins, banknotes and bank deposits subject to check or similar payment on demand (checking accounts)—may be used just like money itself for the settlement of all transactions. Only a part of these money substitutes, however, is fully covered by stocks of gold on deposit in the banks' reserves. In the decades of which we speak, the use of money substitutes has increased considerably more than has the rise in the demand for money and, at the same time, its reserve ratio has worsened. As a result, in spite of an appreciable increase in the demand for money, the demand for gold has not risen enough for the market to absorb the new quantities of gold flowing from production without lowering its purchasing power.

2.   Economizing on Money

If one complains of the decline in the purchasing power of gold today, and contemplates the creation of a monetary unit whose purchasing power shall be more constant than that of gold in recent decades, it should not be forgotten that the principal cause of the decline in the value of gold during this period is to be found in monetary policy and not in gold production itself. Money substitutes not covered by gold, which we call fiduciary media, occupy a relatively more important position today in the world's total quantity of money[2] than in earlier years. But this is not a development which would have taken place without the cooperation, or even without the express support, of governmental monetary policies. As a matter of fact, it was monetary policy itself which was deliberately aimed at a "saving" of gold and which created, thereby, the conditions that led inevitably to the depreciation of gold.

    The fact that we use as money a commodity like gold, which is produced only with a considerable expenditure of capital and labor, saddles mankind with certain costs. If the amount of capital and labor spent for the production of monetary gold could be released and used in other ways, people could be better supplied with goods for their immediate needs. There is no doubt about that! However, it should be noted that, in return for this expenditure, we receive the advantage of having available, for settling transactions, a money with a relatively steady value and, what is more important, the value of which is not directly influenced by governments and political parties. However, it is easy to understand why men began to ponder the possibility of creating

---

2. The quantity of "money in the broader sense" is equal to the quantity of money proper [i.e., commodity money] plus the quantity of fiduciary media [i.e., notes, bank deposits not backed by metal, and subsidiary coins.]

a monetary system that would combine all the advantages offered by the gold standard with the added virtue of lower costs.

Adam Smith drew a parallel between the gold and silver which circulated in a land as money and a highway on which nothing grew, but over which fodder and grain were brought to market. The substitution of notes for the precious metals would create, so to speak, a "waggon-way through the air," making it possible to convert a large part of the roads into fields and pastures and, thus, to increase considerably the yearly output of the economy. Then in 1816, Ricardo devised his famous plan for a gold exchange standard. According to his proposal, England should retain the gold standard, which had proved its value in every respect. However, gold coins should be replaced in domestic trade by banknotes, and these notes should be redeemable, not in gold coins, but in bullion only. Thus the notes would be assured of a value equivalent to that of gold and the country would have the advantage of possessing a monetary standard with all the attributes of the gold standard but at a lower cost.

Ricardo's proposals were not put into effect for decades. As a matter of fact, they were even forgotten. Nevertheless, the gold exchange standard was adopted by a number of countries during the 1890's—in the beginning usually as a temporary expedient only, without intending to direct monetary policy on to a new course. Today it is so widespread that we would be fully justified in describing it as "the monetary standard of our age."[3] However, in a majority, or at least in quite a number of these countries, the gold exchange standard has undergone a development which entitles it to be spoken of rather as a flexible gold exchange standard. Under Ricardo's plan, savings would be realized not only by avoiding the costs of coinage and the loss from wearing coins thin in use, but also because the amount of gold required for circulation and bank reserves would be less than under the "pure" gold standard.

Carrying out this plan in a single country must obviously, *ceteris paribus*, reduce the purchasing power of gold. And the more widely the system was adopted, the more must the purchasing power of gold decline. If a single land adopts the gold exchange standard, while others maintain a "pure" gold standard, then the gold exchange standard country can gain an immediate advantage over costs in the other areas.

3. Machlup, Fritz. *Die Goldkernwährung.* Halberstadt, 1925, p. xi.

The gold which is surplus under the gold exchange standard, as compared with the gold which would have been called for under the "pure" gold standard, may be spent abroad for other commodities. These additional commodities represent an improvement in the country's welfare as a result of introducing the gold exchange standard. The gold exchange standard renders all the services of the gold standard to this country and also brings an additional advantage in the form of this increase of goods.

However, should every country in the world shift at the same time from the "pure" gold standard to a similar gold exchange standard, no gain of this kind would be possible. The distribution of gold throughout the world would remain unchanged. There would be no country where one could exchange a quantity of gold, made superfluous by the adoption of the new monetary system, for other goods. Embracing the new standard would result only in a universally more severe reduction in the purchasing power of gold. This monetary depreciation, like every change in the value of money, would bring about dislocations in the relationships of wealth and income of the various individuals in the economy. As a result, it could also lead indirectly, under certain circumstances, to an increase in capital accumulation. However, this indirect method will make the world richer only insofar as (1) the demand for gold for other uses (industrial and similar purposes) can be better satisfied and (2) a decline in profitability leads to a restriction of gold production and so releases capital and labor for other purposes.

3.   Interest on "Idle" Reserves

In addition to these attempts toward "economy" in the operation of the gold standard, by reducing the domestic demand for gold, other efforts have also aimed at the same objective. Holding gold reserves is costly to the banks of issue because of the loss of interest. Consequently, it was but a short step to the reduction of these costs by permitting non-interest-bearing gold reserves in bank vaults to be replaced by interest-bearing credit balances abroad, payable in gold on demand, and by bills of exchange payable in gold. Assets of this type enable the banks of issue to satisfy demands for gold in foreign trade just as the possession of a stock of gold coins and bars would. As a matter of fact, the dealer in arbitrage who presents notes for redemption will prefer payment in the form of checks, and bills of exchange—foreign financial paper—to redemption in gold because the costs of shipping foreign financial papers are lower than those for the transport of gold. The banks of smaller and poorer lands especially converted a part of their reserves into foreign bills of exchange. The inducement was particularly strong in countries on the gold exchange standard, where the banks did not have to consider a demand for gold for use in domestic circulation. In this way, the gold exchange standard [Goldkernwährung] became the flexible gold exchange standard [Golddevisenkernwährung], i.e., the flexible standard.

Nevertheless, the goal of this policy was not only to reduce the costs involved in the maintenance and circulation of an actual stock of gold. In many countries, including Germany and Austria, this was thought to be a way to reduce the rate of interest. The influence of the Currency Theory had led, decades earlier, to banking legislation intended to avoid the consequences of a paper money inflation. These laws, limiting the issue of banknotes not covered by gold, were still in force. Reared in the Historical-Realistic School of economic thinking, the new generation, insofar as it dealt with these problems, was under the spell of the Banking Theory, and thus no longer understood the meaning of these laws.

Lack of originality prevented the new generation from embarking upon any startling reversal in policy. In line with currently prevailing opinion, it abolished the limitation on the issue of banknotes not covered by metal. The old laws were allowed to stay on the books essentially unchanged. However, various attempts were made to reduce their effect. The most noteworthy of these measures was to encourage, systematically and purposefully, the settlement of transactions without the use of cash. By supplanting cash transactions with checks and other transfer payments, it was expected not only that there would be a reduction in the demand for banknotes but also a flow of gold coins back to the bank and, consequently, a strengthening of the bank's cash position. As German, and also Austrian, banking legislation prescribed a certain percentage of gold cover for notes issued, gold flowing back to the bank meant that more notes could be issued—up to three times their gold value in Germany and two and a half times in Austria. During recent decades, the banking theory has been characterized by a belief that this should result in a reduction in the rate of interest.

4.   Gold Still Money

If we glance, even briefly, at the efforts of monetary and banking policy in recent years, it becomes obvious that the depreciation of gold may be traced in large part to political measures. The decline in the purchasing power of gold and the continual increase in the gold price of all goods and services were not natural phenomena. They were consequences of an economic policy which aimed, to be sure, at other objectives, but which necessarily led to these results. As has already been mentioned, accurate quantitative observations about these matters can never be made. Nevertheless, it is obvious that the increase in gold production has certainly not been the cause, or at least not the only cause, of the depreciation of gold that has been observed since 1896. The policy directed toward displacing gold in actual circulation, which aimed at substituting the gold exchange standard and the flexible standard for the older "pure" gold standard, forced the value of gold down or at least helped to depress it. Perhaps, if this policy had not been followed, we would hear complaints today over the increase, rather than the depreciation, in the value of gold.

Gold has not been demonetized by the new monetary policy, as silver was a short time ago, for it remains the basis of our entire monetary system. Gold is still, as it was formerly, our money. There is no basis for saying that it has been de-throned, as suggested by scatterbrained innovators of catchwords and slogans who want to cure the world of the "money illusion." Nevertheless, gold has been removed from actual use in transactions by the public at large. It has disappeared from view and has been concentrated in bank vaults and monetary reserves. Gold has been taken out of common use and this must necessarily tend to lower its value.

It is wrong to point to the general price increases of recent years to illustrate the inadequacy of the gold standard. It is not the old style gold standard, as recommended by advocates of the gold standard in England and Germany, which has given us a monetary system that has led to rising prices in recent years. Rather these price increases have been the results of monetary and banking policies which permitted the "pure" or "classical" gold standard to be replaced by the gold exchange and flexible standards, leaving in circulation only notes and small coins and concentrating the gold stocks in bank and currency reserves.

III

The "Manipulation" of the Gold Standard

1. Monetary Policy and Purchasing Power of Gold

Most important for the old, "pure," or classical gold standard, as originally formulated in England and later, after the formation of the Empire, adopted in Germany, was the fact that it made the formation of prices independent of political influence and the shifting views which sway political action. This feature especially recommended the gold standard to liberals who feared that economic productivity might be impaired as a result of the tendency of governments to favor certain groups of persons at the expense of others.

However, it should certainly not be forgotten that under the "pure" gold standard governmental measures may also have a significant influence on the formation of the value of gold. In the first place, governmental actions determine whether to adopt the gold standard, abandon it, or return to it. However, the effect of these governmental actions, which we need not consider any further here, is conceived as very different from those described by the various "state theories of money"—theories which, now at long last, are generally recognized as absurd. The continual displacement of the silver standard by the gold standard and the shift in some countries from credit money to gold added to the demand for monetary gold in the years before the World War [1914–1918]. War measures resulted in monetary policies that led the belligerent nations, as well as some neutral states, to release large parts of their gold reserves, thus releasing more gold for world markets. Every political act in this area, insofar as it affects the demand for, and the quantity of, gold as money, represents a "manipulation" of the gold standard and affects all countries adhering to the gold standard.

Just as the "pure" gold, the gold exchange and the flexible standards do not differ in principle, but only in the degree to which money substitutes are actually used in circulation, so is there no basic difference in their susceptibility to manipulation. The "pure" gold standard is subject to the influence of monetary measures—on the one hand, insofar as monetary policy may affect the acceptance or rejection of the gold standard in a political area and, on the other hand, insofar as monetary policy, while still clinging to the gold standard in principle, may bring about changes in the demand for gold through an increase or decrease in actual gold circulation or by changes in reserve requirements for banknotes and checking accounts. The influence of monetary policy on the formation of the value [i.e., the purchasing power] of gold also extends just that far and no farther under the gold exchange and flexible standards. Here again, governments and those agencies responsible for monetary policy can influence the formation of the value of gold by changing the course of monetary policy. The extent of this influence depends on how large the increase or decrease in the demand for gold is nationally, in relation to the total world demand for gold.

If advocates of the old "pure" gold standard spoke of the independence of the value of gold from governmental influences, they meant that once the gold standard had been adopted everywhere (and gold standard advocates of the last three decades of the nineteenth century had not the slightest doubt that this would soon come to pass, for the gold standard had already been almost universally accepted) no further political action would affect the formation of monetary value. This would be equally true for both the gold exchange and flexible standards. It would by no means disturb the logical assumptions of the perceptive "pure" gold standard advocate to say that the value of gold would be considerably affected by a change in United States Federal Reserve Board policy, such as the resumption of the circulation of gold or the retention of larger gold reserves in European countries. In this sense, all monetary standards may be "manipulated" under today's economic conditions. The advantage of the gold standard—whether "pure" or "gold exchange"—is due solely to the fact that, if once generally adopted in a definite form, and adhered to, it is no longer subject to specific political interferences.

War and postwar actions, with respect to monetary policy, have radically changed the monetary situation throughout the entire world. One by one, individual countries are now [1928] reverting to a gold basis and it is likely that this process will soon be completed. Now, this leads to a second problem: Should the exchange standard, which generally prevails today, be retained? Or should a return be made once more to the actual use of gold in moderate-sized transactions as before under the "pure" gold standard? Also, if it is decided to remain on the exchange standard, should reserves actually be maintained in gold? And at what height? Or could individual countries be satisfied with reserves of foreign exchange payable in gold? (Obviously, the flexible standard cannot become entirely universal. At least one country must continue to invest its reserves in real gold, even if it does not use gold in actual circulation.) Only if the state of affairs prevailing at a given instant in every single area is maintained and, also, only if matters are left just as they are, including of course the ratio of bank reserves, can it be said that the gold standard cannot be manipulated in the manner described above. If these problems are dealt with in such a way as to change markedly the demand for gold for monetary purposes, then the purchasing power of gold must undergo corresponding changes.

To repeat for the sake of clarity, this represents no essential disagreement with the advocates of the gold standard as to what they considered its special superiority. Changes in the monetary system of any large and wealthy land will necessarily influence substantially the creation of monetary value. Once these changes have been carried out and have worked their effect on the purchasing power of gold, the value of money will necessarily be affected again by a return to the previous monetary system. However, this detracts in no way from the truth of the statement that the creation of value under the gold standard is independent of politics, so long as no essential changes are made in its structure, nor in the size of the area where it prevails.

2. Changes in Purchasing Power of Gold

Irving Fisher, as well as many others, criticize the gold standard because the purchasing power of gold has declined considerably since 1896, and especially since 1914. In order to avoid misunderstanding, it should be pointed out that this drop in the purchasing power of gold must be traced back to monetary policy—monetary policy which fostered the reduction in the purchasing power of gold through measures adopted between 1896 and 1914, to "economize" gold and, since 1914, through the rejection of gold as the basis for money in many countries. If others denounce the gold standard because the imminent return to

the actual use of gold in circulation and the strengthening of gold reserves in countries on the exchange standard would bring about an
increase in the purchasing power of gold, then it becomes obvious that
we are dealing with the consequences of political changes in monetary
policy which transform the structure of the gold standard.

The purchasing power of gold is not "stable." It should be pointed
out that there is no such thing as "stable" purchasing power, and never
can be. The concept of "stable value" is vague and indistinct. Strictly
speaking, only an economy in the final state of rest—where all prices
remain unchanged—could have a money with fixed purchasing power.
However, it is a fact which no one can dispute that the gold standard,
once generally adopted and adhered to without changes, makes the formation of the purchasing power of gold independent of the operations
of shifting political efforts.

As gold is obtained only from a few sources, which sooner or later
will be exhausted, the fear is repeatedly expressed that there may someday be a scarcity of gold and, as a consequence, a continuing decline
in commodity prices. Such fears became especially great in the late
1870's and the 1880's. Then they quieted down. Only in recent years
have they been revived again. Calculations are made indicating that
the placers and mines currently being worked will be exhausted within
the foreseeable future. No prospects are seen that any new rich sources
of gold will be opened up. Should the demand for money increase in
the future, to the same extent as it has in the recent past, then a general
price drop appears inevitable, if we remain on the gold standard.[1]

Now one must be very cautious with forecasts of this kind. A half
century ago, Eduard Suess, the geologist, claimed—and he sought to
establish this scientifically—that an unavoidable decline in gold production should be expected.[2] Facts very soon proved him wrong. And it
may be that those who express similar ideas today will also be refuted
just as quickly and just as thoroughly. Still we must agree that they
are right in the final analysis, that prices are tending to fall [1928] and
that all the social consequences of an increase in purchasing power are
making their appearance. What may be ventured, given the circumstances, in order to change the economic pessimism, will be discussed
at the end of the second part of this study.

1. Cassell, Gustav. *Währungsstabilisierung als Weltproblem.* Leipzig, 1928, p. 12.
2. [Eduard Suess (1831–1914) published a study in German (1877) on "The Future of
Gold."—Ed.]

IV

"Measuring" Changes in the Purchasing Power of the Monetary Unit

1. Imaginary Constructions

All proposals to replace the commodity money, gold, with a money thought to be better, because it is more "stable" in value, are based on the vague idea that changes in purchasing power can somehow be measured. Only by starting from such an assumption is it possible to conceive of a monetary unit with unchanging purchasing power as the ideal and to consider seeking ways to reach this goal. These proposals, vague and basically contradictory, are derived from the old, long since exploded, objective theory of value. Yet they are not even completely consistent with that theory. They now appear very much out of place in the company of modern subjective economics.

The prestige which they still enjoy can be explained only by the fact that, until very recently, studies in subjective economics have been restricted to the theory of direct exchange (barter). Only lately have such studies been expanded to include also the theory of intermediate (indirect) exchange, i.e., the theory of a generally accepted medium of exchange (Monetary Theory) and the theory of fiduciary media (Banking Theory) with all their relevant problems.[1] It is certainly high time to expose conclusively the errors and defects of the basic concept that purchasing power can be measured.

Exchange ratios on the market are constantly subject to change. If we imagine a market where no generally accepted medium of exchange, i.e., no money, is used, it is easy to recognize how nonsensical the idea is of trying to measure the changes taking place in exchange ratios. It is

---

1. *The Theory of Money and Credit* [(Yale, 1953), pp. 97ff.; (Liberty Fund, 1981), pp. 117ff.—Ed.].

only if we resort to the fiction of completely stationary exchange ratios among all commodities, other than money, and then compare these other commodities with money, that we can envisage exchange relationships between money and each of the other individual exchange commodities changing uniformly. Only then can we speak of a uniform increase or decrease in the monetary price of all commodities and of a uniform rise or fall of the "price level." Still, we must not forget that this concept is pure fiction, what Vaihinger termed an "as if."[2] It is a deliberate imaginary construction, indispensable for scientific thinking.

Perhaps the necessity for this imaginary construction will become somewhat more clear if we express it, not in terms of the objective exchange value of the market, but in terms of the subjective exchange valuation of the acting individual. To do that, we must imagine an unchanging man with never-changing values. Such an individual could determine, from his never-changing scale of values, the purchasing power of money. He could say precisely how the quantity of money, which he must spend to attain a certain amount of satisfaction, had changed. Nevertheless, the idea of a definite structure of prices, a "price level," which is raised or lowered uniformly, is just as fictitious as this. However, it enables us to recognize clearly that every change in the exchange ratio between a commodity, on the one side, and money, on the other, must necessarily lead to shifts in the disposition of wealth and income among acting individuals. Thus, each such change acts as a dynamic agent also. In view of this situation, therefore, it is not permissible to make such an assumption as a uniformly changing "level" of prices.

This imaginary construction is necessary, however, to explain that the exchange ratios of the various economic goods may undergo a change from the side of one individual commodity. This fictional concept is the *ceteris paribus* of the theory of exchange relationships. It is just as fictitious and, at the same time, just as indispensable as any *ceteris paribus*. If extraordinary circumstances lead to exceptionally large and hence conspicuous changes in exchange ratios, data on market phenomena may help to facilitate sound thinking on these problems. However, then even more than ever, if we want to see the situation at all clearly, we must resort to the imaginary construction necessary for an understanding of our theory.

The expressions "inflation" and "deflation," scarcely known in Ger-

---

2. [Hans Vaihinger (1852–1933), author of *The Philosophy of As If* (German, 1911; English translation, 1924).—Ed.]

man economic literature several years ago, are in daily use today. In spite of their inexactness, they are undoubtedly suitable for general use in public discussions of economic and political problems.[3] But in order to understand them precisely, one must elaborate with rigid logic that fictional concept [the imaginary construction of completely stationary exchange ratios among all commodities other than money], the falsity of which is clearly recognized.

Among the significant services performed by this fiction is that it enables us to distinguish and determine whether changes in exchange relationships between money and other commodities arise on the money side or the commodity side. In order to understand the changes which take place constantly on the market, this distinction is urgently needed. It is still more indispensable for judging the significance of measures proposed or adopted in the field of monetary and banking policy. Even in these cases, however, we can never succeed in constructing a fictional representation that coincides with the situation which actually appears on the market. The imaginary construction makes it easier to understand reality, but we must remain conscious of the distinction between fiction and reality.[4]

3. *The Theory of Money and Credit* [(Yale, 1953), pp. 239ff.; (Liberty Fund, 1981), pp. 271ff.—Ed.].

4. Carl Menger referred to the nature and extent of the influence exerted on money/goods exchange ratios [prices] by changes from the money side as the problem of the "internal" exchange value (*innere Tauschwert*) of money [translated in this volume as "cash-induced changes"]. He referred to the variations in the purchasing power of the monetary unit due to other causes as changes in the "external" exchange value (*aussere Tauschwert*) of money [translated as "goods-induced changes"]. I have criticized both expressions as being rather unfortunate—because of possible confusion with the terms "extrinsic and intrinsic value" as used in Roman canon doctrine, and by English authors of the seventeenth and eighteenth centuries. (See the German editions of my book on *The Theory of Money and Credit*, 1912, p. 132; 1924, p. 104). Nevertheless, this terminology has attained scientific acceptance through its use by Menger and it will be used in this study when appropriate.

There is no need to discuss an expression which describes a useful and indispensable idea. It is the concept itself, not the term used to describe it, which is important. Serious mischief is done if an author chooses a new term unnecessarily to express a concept for which a name already exists. My student, Gottfried Haberler, has criticized me severely for taking this position, reproaching me for being a slave to semantics. (See Haberler, *Der Sinn der Indexzahlen*, Tübingen, 1927, pp. 109ff.). However, in his relevant remarks on this problem, Haberler says nothing more than I have. He too distinguishes between price changes arising on the goods and money sides. Beginners should seek to expand knowledge and avoid spending time on useless terminological disputes. As Haberler points out, it would obviously be wasted effort to "seek internal and external exchange values of money in the real world." Ideas do not belong to the "real world" at all, but to the world of thought and knowledge.

It is even more astonishing that Haberler finds my critique of attempts to measure the value of the monetary unit "inexpedient," especially as his analysis rests entirely on mine.

2.   Index Numbers

Attempts have been made to measure changes in the purchasing power of money by using data derived from changes in the money prices of individual economic goods. These attempts rest on the theory that, in a carefully selected index of a large number, or of all, consumers' goods, influences from the commodity side affecting commodity prices cancel each other out. Thus, so the theory goes, the direction and extent of the influence on prices of factors arising on the money side may be discovered from such an index. Essentially, therefore, by computing an arithmetical mean, this method seeks to convert the price changes emerging among the various consumers' goods into a figure which may then be considered an index to the change in the value of money. In this discussion, we shall disregard the practical difficulties which arise in assembling the price quotations necessary to serve as the basis for such calculations and restrict ourselves to commenting on the fundamental usefulness of this method for the solution of our problem.

First of all it should be noted that there are various arithmetical means. Which one should be selected? That is an old question. Reasons may be advanced for, and objections raised against, each. From our point of view, the only important thing to be learned in such a debate is that the question cannot be settled conclusively so that everyone will accept any single answer as "right."

The other fundamental question concerns the relative importance of the various consumer goods. In developing the index, if the price of each and every commodity is considered as having the same weight, a 50% increase in the price of bread, for instance, would be offset in calculating the arithmetical average by a drop of one-half in the price of diamonds. The index would then indicate no change in purchasing power, or "price level." As such a conclusion is obviously preposterous, attempts are made in fabricating index numbers, to use the prices of various commodities according to their relative importance. Prices should be included in the calculations according to the coefficient of their importance. The result is then known as a "weighted" average.

This brings us to the second arbitrary decision necessary for developing such an index. What is "importance"? Several different approaches have been tried and arguments pro and con each have been raised. Obviously, a clear-cut, all-round satisfactory solution to the problem cannot be found. Special attention has been given the difficulty arising from the fact that, if the usual method is followed, the very circumstances involved in determining "importance" are constantly in flux; thus the coefficient of importance itself is also continuously changing.

As soon as one starts to take into consideration the "importance" of the various goods, one forsakes the assumption of objective exchange value—which often leads to nonsensical conclusions as pointed out above—and enters the area of subjective values. Since there is no generally recognized immutable "importance" to various goods, since "subjective" value has meaning only from the point of view of the acting individual, further reflection leads eventually to the subjective method already discussed—namely the inexcusable fiction of a never-changing man with never-changing values. To avoid arriving at this conclusion, which is also obviously absurd, one remains indecisively on the fence, midway between two equally nonsensical methods—on the one side the unweighted average and on the other the fiction of a never-changing individual with never-changing values. Yet one believes he has discovered something useful. Truth is not the halfway point between two untruths. The fact that each of these two methods, if followed to its logical conclusion, is shown to be preposterous, in no way proves that a combination of the two is the correct one.

All index computations pass quickly over these unanswerable objections. The calculations are made with whatever coefficients of importance are selected. However, we have established that even the problem of determining "importance" is not capable of solution, with certainty, in such a way as to be recognized by everyone as "right."

Thus the idea that changes in the purchasing power of money may be measured is scientifically untenable. This will come as no surprise to anyone who is acquainted with the fundamental problems of modern subjectivistic catallactics and has recognized the significance of recent studies with respect to the measurement of value[5] and the meaning of monetary calculation.[6]

One can certainly try to devise index numbers. Nowadays nothing is more popular among statisticians than this. Nevertheless, all these computations rest on a shaky foundation. Disregarding entirely the difficulties which, from time to time, even thwart agreement as to the commodities whose prices will form the basis of these calculations,

5. See *The Theory of Money and Credit* [(yale, 1953), pp. 38ff.; (Liberty Fund, 1981), pp. 51ff.—Ed.].
6. See *Socialism* [(Yale, 1951), pp. 114ff.; (Liberty Fund, 1981), pp. 97ff.—Ed.].

these computations are arbitrary in two ways—first, with respect to the arithmetical mean chosen and, secondly, with respect to the coefficient of importance selected. There is no way to characterize one of the many possible methods as the only "correct" one and the others as "false." Each is equally legitimate or illegitimate. None is scientifically meaningful.

It is small consolation to point out that the results of the various methods do not differ substantially from one another. Even if that is the case, it cannot in the least affect the conclusions we must draw from the observations we have made. The fact that people can conceive of such a scheme at all, that they are not more critical, may be explained only by the eventuality of the great inflations, especially the greatest and most recent one.

Any index method is good enough to make a rough statement about the extremely severe depreciation of the value of a monetary unit, such as that wrought in the German [1923] inflation. There, the index served an instructional task, enlightening a people who were inclined to the "State Theory of Money" idea. Nevertheless, a method that helps to open the eyes of the people is not necessarily either scientifically correct or applicable in actual practice.

V

Fisher's Stabilization Plan

1.   Political Problem

The superiority of the gold standard consists in the fact that the value of gold develops independent of political actions. It is clear that its value is not "stable." There is not, and never can be, any such thing as stability of value. If, under a "manipulated" monetary standard, it was government's task to influence the value of money, the question of how this influence was to be exercised would soon become the main issue among political and economic interests. Government would be asked to influence the purchasing power of money so that certain politically powerful groups would be favored by its intervention, at the expense of the rest of the population. Intense political battles would rage over the direction and scope of the edicts affecting monetary policy. At times, steps would be taken in one direction, and at other times in other directions—in response to the momentary balance of political power. The steady, progressive development of the economy would continually experience disturbances from the side of money. The result of the manipulation would be to provide us with a monetary system which would certainly not be any more stable than the gold standard.

If the decision were made to alter the purchasing power of money so that the index number always remained unchanged, the situation would not be any different. We have seen that there are many possible ways, not just one single way, to determine the index number. No single one of these methods can be considered the only correct one. Moreover, each leads to a different conclusion. Each political party would advocate the index method which promised results consistent with its political aims at the time. Since it is not scientifically possible to find one of the many methods objectively right and to reject all others as false, no judge could decide impartially among groups disputing the correct method of calculation.

In addition, however, there is still one more very important consideration. The early proponents of the Quantity Theory believed that changes in the purchasing power of the monetary unit caused by a change in the quantity of money were exactly inversely proportional to one another. According to this Theory, a doubling of the quantity of money would cut the monetary unit's purchasing power in half. It is to the credit of the more recently developed monetary theory that this version of the Quantity Theory has been proved untenable. An increase in the quantity of money must, to be sure, lead *ceteris paribus* to a decline in the purchasing power of the monetary unit. Still the extent of this decrease in no way corresponds to the extent of the increase in the quantity of money. No fixed quantitative relationship can be established between the changes in the quantity of money and those of the unit's purchasing power.[1] Hence, every manipulation of the monetary standard will lead to serious difficulties. Political controversies would arise not only over the "need" for a measure, but also over the degree of inflation or restriction, even after agreement had been reached on the purpose the measure was supposed to serve.

All this is sufficient to explain why proposals for establishing a manipulated standard have not been popular. It also explains—even if one disregards the way finance ministers have abused their authority—why credit money (commonly known as "paper money") is considered "bad" money. Credit money is considered "bad money" precisely because it may be manipulated.

2.   Multiple Commodity Standard

Proposals that a multiple commodity standard replace, or supplement, monetary standards based on the precious metals—in their role as standards of deferred payments—are by no means intended to create a manipulated money. They are not intended to change the precious metals standard itself nor its effect on value. They seek merely to provide a way to free all transactions involving future monetary payments from

1. See *The Theory of Money and Credit* [(Yale, 1953), pp. 139ff.; (Liberty Fund, 1981,) pp. 161ff.—Ed.].

the effect of changes in the value of the monetary unit. It is easy to understand why these proposals were not put into practice. Relying as they do on the shaky foundation of index number calculations, which cannot be scientifically established, they would not have produced a stable standard of value for deferred payments. They would only have created a different standard with different changes in value from those under the gold metallic standard.

To some extent Fisher's proposals parallel the early ideas of advocates of a multiple commodity standard. These forerunners also tried to eliminate only the influence of the social effects of changes in monetary value on the content of future monetary obligations. Like most Anglo-American students of this problem, as well as earlier advocates of a multiple commodity standard, Fisher took little notice of the fact that changes in the value of money have *other* social effects also.

Fisher, too, based his proposals entirely on index numbers. What seems to recommend *his* scheme, as compared with proposals for introducing a "multiple standard," is the fact that he does not use index numbers directly to determine changes in purchasing power over a long period of time. Rather he uses them primarily to understand changes taking place from month to month only. Many objections raised against the use of the index method for analyzing longer periods of time will perhaps appear less justified when considering only shorter periods. But there is no need to discuss this question here, for Fisher did *not* confine the application of his plan to short periods only. Also, even if adjustments are always made from month to month only, they were to be carried forward, on and on, until eventually calculations were being made, with the help of the index number, which extended over long periods of time. Because of the imperfection of the index number, these calculations would necessarily lead in time to errors of very considerable proportions.

3.   Price Premium

Fisher's most important contribution to monetary theory is the emphasis he gave to the previously little noted effect of changes in the value of money on the formation of the interest rate.[2] Insofar as move-

---

2. Fisher, Irving. *The Rate of Interest*. New York, 1907, pp. 77ff.

ments in the purchasing power of money can be foreseen, they find expression in the gross interest rate—not only as to the direction they will take but also as to their approximate magnitude. That portion of the gross interest rate which is demanded, and granted, in view of anticipated changes in purchasing power is known as the purchasing-power-change premium or price-change premium. In place of these clumsy expressions we shall use a shorter term—"price premium." Without any further explanation, this terminology leads to an understanding of the fact that, given an anticipation of general price increases, the price premium is "positive," thus raising the gross rate of interest. On the other hand, with an anticipation of general price *decreases*, the price premium becomes "negative" and so reduces the gross interest rate.

The individual businessman is not generally aware of the fact that monetary value is affected by changes from the side of money. Even if he were, the difficulties which hamper the formation of a halfway reliable judgment, as to the direction and extent of anticipated changes, are tremendous, if, not outright insurmountable. Consequently, monetary units used in credit transactions are generally regarded rather naively as being "stable" in value. So, with agreement as to conditions under which credit will be applied for and granted, a price premium is not generally considered in the calculation. This is practically always true, even for long-term credit. If opinion is shaken as to the "stability of value" of a certain kind of money, this money is not used at all in long-term credit transactions. Thus, in all nations using credit money, whose purchasing power fluctuated violently, long-term credit obligations were drawn up in gold, whose value was held to be "stable."

However, because of obstinacy and pro-government bias, this course of action was not employed in Germany, nor in other countries during the recent inflation. Instead, the idea was conceived of making loans in terms of rye and potash. If there had been no hope at all of a later compensating revaluation of these loans, their price on the exchange in German marks, Austrian crowns and similarly inflated currencies would have been so high that a positive price premium corresponding to the magnitude of the anticipated further depreciation of these currencies would have been reflected in the actual interest payment.

The situation is different with respect to short-term credit transactions. Every businessman estimates the price changes anticipated in the immediate future and guides himself accordingly in making sales and purchases. If he expects an increase in prices, he will make purchases and postpone sales. To secure the means for carrying out this plan, he will be ready to offer higher interest than otherwise. If he expects a drop in prices, then he will seek to sell and to refrain from purchasing. He will then be prepared to lend out, at a cheaper rate, the money made available as a result. Thus, the expectation of price increases leads to a positive price premium, that of price declines to a negative price premium.

To the extent that this process correctly anticipates the price movements that actually result, with respect to short-term credit, it cannot very well be maintained that the content of contractual obligations is transformed by the change in the purchasing power of money in a way which was neither foreseen nor contemplated by the parties concerned. Nor can it be maintained that, as a result, shifts take place in the wealth and income relationship between creditor and debtor. Consequently, it is unnecessary, so far as short-term credit is concerned, to look for a more perfect standard of deferred payments.

Thus we are in a position to see that Fisher's proposal actually offers no more than was offered by any previous plan for a multiple standard. In regard to the role of money as a standard of deferred payments, the verdict must be that, for long-term contracts, Fisher's scheme is inadequate. For short-term commitments, it is both inadequate and superfluous.

4. Changes in Wealth and Income

However, the social consequences of changes in the value of money are not limited to altering the content of future monetary obligations. In addition to these social effects, which are generally the only ones dealt with in Anglo-American literature, there are still others. Changes in money prices never reach all commodities at the same time, and they do not affect the prices of the various goods to the same extent. Shifts in relationships between the demand for, and the quantity of, money for cash holdings generated by changes in the value of money from the money side do not appear simultaneously and uniformly throughout the entire economy. They must necessarily appear on the market at some definite point, affecting only one group in the economy at first, influencing only *their* judgments of value in the beginning and, as a result, only the prices of commodities these particular persons are demanding. Only gradually does the change in the purchasing power of the monetary unit make its way throughout the entire economy.

For example, if the quantity of money increases, the additional new quantity of money must necessarily flow first of all into the hands of certain definite individuals—gold producers, for example, or, in the case of paper money inflation, the coffers of the government. It changes only *their* incomes and fortunes at first and, consequently, only *their* value judgments. Not all goods go up in price in the beginning, but only those goods which are demanded by these first beneficiaries of the inflation. Only later are prices of the remaining goods raised, as the increased quantity of money progresses step by step throughout the land and eventually reaches every participant in the economy.[3] But even then, when finally the upheaval of prices due to the new quantity of money has ended, the prices of all goods and services will not have increased to the same extent. Precisely because the price increases have not affected all commodities at one time, shifts in the relationships in wealth and income are effected which affect the supply and demand of individual goods and services differently. Thus, these shifts must lead to a new orientation of the market and of market prices.

Suppose we ignore the consequences of changes in the value of money on future monetary obligations. Suppose further that changes in the purchasing power of money occur simultaneously and uniformly with respect to all commodities in the entire economy. Then, it becomes obvious that changes in the value of money would produce no changes in the wealth of the individual entrepreneurs. Changes in the value of the monetary unit would then have no more significance for them than changes in weights and measures or in the calendar.

It is only because changes in the purchasing power of money never affect all commodities everywhere simultaneously that they bring with them (in addition to their influence on debt transactions) still other shifts in wealth and income. The groups which produce and sell the commodities that go up in price first are benefited by the inflation, for they realize higher profits in the beginning and yet they can still buy the commodities they need at lower prices, reflecting the previous stock of money. So during the inflation of the World War [1914–1918],

---

3. Gossen, Hermann Heinrich. *Entwicklung der Gesetze des menschlichen Verkehrs und der daraus fliessenden Regeln für menschliches Handeln* (new ed.). Berlin, 1889, p. 206.

the producers of war materiel and the workers in war industries, who received the output of the printing presses earlier than other groups of people, benefited from the monetary depreciation. At the same time, those whose incomes remained nominally the same suffered from the inflation, as they were forced to compete in making purchases with those receiving war inflated incomes. The situation became especially clear in the case of government employees. There was no mistaking the fact that they were losers. Salary increases came to them too late. For some time they had to pay prices, already affected by the increase in the quantity of money, with money incomes related to previous conditions.

5.   Uncompensatable Changes

In the case of foreign trade, it was just as easy to see the consequences of the fact that price changes of the various commodities did not take place simultaneously. The deterioration in the value of the monetary unit encourages exports because a part of the raw materials, semi-produced factors of production and labor needed for the manufacture of export commodities, were procured at the old lower prices. At the same time the change in purchasing power, which for the time being has affected only a part of the domestically-produced commodities, has already had an influence on the rate of exchange on the Bourse. The result is that the exporter realizes a specific monetary gain.

The changes in purchasing power arising on the money side are considered disturbing not merely because of the transformation they bring about in the content of future monetary obligations. They are also upsetting because of the uneven timing of the price changes of the various goods and services. Can Fisher's dollar of "stable value" eliminate *these* price changes?

In order to answer this question, it must be restated that Fisher's proposal does not eliminate changes in the value of the monetary unit. It attempts instead to compensate for these changes continuously—from month to month. Thus the consequences associated with the step-by-step emergence of changes in purchasing power are not eliminated. Rather they materialize during the course of the month. Then, when the correction is made at the end of the month, the course of monetary depreciation is still not ended. The adjustment calculated at that time is based on the index number of the *previous* month when the full extent of that month's monetary depreciation had not then been felt because all prices had not yet been affected. However, the prices of goods for which demand was forced up first by the additional quantity of money undoubtedly reached heights that may not be maintained later.

Whether or not these two deviations in prices correspond in such a way that their effects cancel each other out will depend on the specific data in each individual case. Consequently, the monetary depreciation will continue in the following month, even if no further increase in the quantity of money were to appear in that month. It would continue to go on until the process finally ended with a general increase in commodity prices, in terms of gold, and thus with an increase in the value of the gold dollar on the basis of the index number. The social consequences of the uneven timing of price changes would, therefore, not be avoided because the unequal timing of the price changes of various commodities and services would not have been eliminated.[4]

So there is no need to go into more detail with respect to the technical difficulties that stand in the way of realizing Fisher's Plan. Even if it could be put into operation successfully, it would not provide us with a monetary system that would leave the disposition of wealth and income undisturbed.

---

4. See also my critique of Fisher's proposal in *The Theory of Money and Credit* [(Yale, 1953), pp. 399ff.; (Liberty Fund, 1981), pp. 438ff.—Ed.].

VI

Goods-induced and Cash-induced Changes in the Purchasing Power of the Monetary Unit

1.   The Inherent Instability of Market Ratios

Changes in the exchange ratios between money and the various other commodities may originate either from the money side or from the commodity side of the transaction. Stabilization policy does not aim only at eliminating changes arising on the side of money. It also seeks to prevent all future price changes, even if this is not always clearly expressed and may sometimes be disputed.

It is not necessary for our purposes to go any further into the market phenomena which an increase or decrease in commodities must set in motion if the quantity of money remains unchanged.[1] It is sufficient to point out that, in addition to changes in the exchange ratios among individual commodities, shifts would also appear in the exchange ratios between money and the majority of the other commodities in the market. A decrease in the quantity of other commodities would weaken the purchasing power of the monetary unit. An increase would enhance it. It should be noted, however, that the social adjustments which must result from these changes in the quantity of other commodities will lead to a reorganization in the demand for money and hence cash holdings. These shifts can occur in such a way as to counteract the immediate effect of the change in the quantity of goods on the purchasing power of the monetary unit. Still, for the time being we may ignore this situation.

The goal of all stabilization proposals, as we have seen, is to maintain

---

1. Whether this is considered a change of purchasing power from the money side or from the commodity side is purely a matter of terminology.

unchanged the original content of future monetary obligations. Creditors and debtors should neither gain nor lose in purchasing power. This is assumed to be "just." Of course, what is "just" or "unjust" cannot be scientifically determined. That is a question of ultimate purpose and ethical judgment. It is not a question of fact.

It is impossible to know just why the advocates of purchasing power stabilization see as "just" only the maintenance of an unchanged purchasing power for *future* monetary obligations. However, it is easy to understand that they do not want to permit either debtor or creditor to gain or lose. They want contractual liabilities to continue in force as little altered as possible in the midst of the constantly changing world economy. They want to transplant contractual liabilities out of the flow of events, so to speak, and into a timeless existence.

Now let us see what this means. Imagine that all production has become more fruitful. Goods flow more abundantly than ever before. Where only one unit was available for consumption before, there are now two. Since the quantity of money has not been increased, the purchasing power of the monetary unit has risen and with one monetary unit it is possible to buy, let us say, one and a half times as much merchandise as before. Whether this actually means, if no "stabilization policy" is attempted, that the debtor now has a disadvantage and the creditor an advantage is not immediately clear.

If you look at the situation from the viewpoint of the prices of the factors of production, it is easy to see why this is the case. For the debtor could use the borrowed sum to buy at lower prices factors of production whose output has not gone up; or if their output has gone up, their prices have not risen correspondingly. It might now be possible to buy *for less money* factors of production with a productive capacity comparable to that of the factors of production one could have bought with the borrowed money at the time of the loan. There is no point in exploring the uncertainties of theories which do not take into consideration the influence that ensuing changes exert on entrepreneurial profit, interest and rent.

However, if we consider changes in real income due to increased production, it becomes evident that the situation may be viewed very differently from the way it appears to those who favor "stabilization." If the creditor gets back the same nominal sum, he can obviously buy more goods. Still, his economic situation is not improved as a result. He is not benefited relative to the general increase of real income which has taken place. If the multiple commodity standard were to reduce in part the nominal debt, his economic situation would be worsened. He would be deprived of something that, in his view, in all fairness belonged to him. Under a multiple commodity standard, interest payable over time, life annuities, subsistence allowances, pensions, and the like would be increased or decreased according to the index number. Thus, these considerations cannot be summarily dismissed as irrelevant from the viewpoint of consumers.

We find, on the one hand, that neither the multiple commodity standard nor Irving Fisher's specific proposal is capable of eliminating the economic concomitants of changes in the value of the monetary unit due to the unequal timing in appearance and the irregularity in size of price changes. On the other hand, we see that these proposals seek to eliminate the repercussions on the content of debt agreements, circumstances permitting, in such a way as to cause definite shifts in wealth and income relations, shifts which appear obviously "unjust," at least to those on whom their burden falls. The "justice" of these proposed reforms, therefore, is somewhat more doubtful than their advocates are inclined to assume.

2.   The Misplaced Partiality to Debtors

It is certainly regrettable that this worthy goal cannot be attained, at least not by this particular route. These and similar efforts are usually acknowledged with sympathy by many who recognize their fallacy and their unworkability. This sympathy is based ultimately on the intellectual and physical inclination of men to be both lazy and resistant to change at the same time. Surely everyone wants to see his situation improved with respect to his supply of goods and the satisfaction of his wants. Surely everyone hopes for changes which would make him richer. Many circumstances make it appear that the old and the traditional, being familiar, are preferable to the new. Such circumstances would include distrust of the individual's own powers and abilities, aversion to being forced to adapt in thought and action to new situations and, finally, the knowledge that one is no longer able, in advanced years of life, to meet his obligations with the vitality of youth.

Certainly, something new is welcomed and gratefully accepted, if the something new is beneficial to the individual's welfare. However, any change which brings disadvantages or merely appears to bring them, whether or not the change is to blame, is considered "unjust." Those favored by the new state of affairs through no special merit on their part quietly accept the increased prosperity as a matter of course and even as something already long due. Those hurt by the change, however, complain vociferously. From such observations, there developed the concepts of a "just price" and a "just wage." Whoever fails to keep up with the times and is unable to comply with its demands becomes a eulogist of the past and an advocate of the status quo. However, the ideal of stability, of the stationary economy, is directly opposed to that of continual progress.

For some time popular opinion has been in sympathy with the debtor. The picture of the rich creditor, demanding payment from the poor debtor, and the vindictive teachings of moralists dominate popular thinking on indebtedness. A byproduct of this is to be found in the contrast, made by the contemporaries of the Classical School and their followers, between the "idle rich" and the "industrious poor." However, with the development of bonds and savings deposits, and with the decline of small-scale enterprise and the rise of big business, a reversal of the former situation took place. It then became possible for the masses, with their increasing prosperity, to become creditors. The "rich man" is no longer the typical creditor, nor the "poor man" the typical debtor. In many cases, perhaps even in the majority of cases, the relationship is completely reversed. Today, except in the lands of farmers and small property owners, the debtor viewpoint is no longer that of the masses. Consequently it is also no longer the view of the political demagogues.[2] Once upon a time inflation may have found its strongest support among the masses, who were burdened with debts. But the situation is now very different. A policy of monetary restriction would not be unwelcome among the masses today, for they would hope to reap a sure gain from it as creditors. They would expect the decline in their wages and salaries to lag behind, or at any rate not to exceed, the drop in commodity prices.

It is understandable, therefore, that proposals for the creation of a "stable value" standard of deferred payments, almost completely forgotten in the years when commodity prices were declining, have been re-

2. [Since this was written almost every government has become the largest borrower in its respective country. Thus today's government officials are inclined to the debtor's viewpoint, favoring low interest rates to keep down government interest payments.—Ed.]

vived again in the twentieth century. Proposals of this kind are always primarily intended for the prevention of losses to creditors, hardly ever to safeguard jeopardized debtor interests. They cropped up in England when she was the great world banker. They turned up again in the United States at the moment when she started to become a creditor nation instead of a land of debtors, and they became quite popular there when America became the great world creditor.

Many signs seem to indicate that the period of monetary depreciation is coming to an end. Should this actually be the case, then the appeal which the idea of a manipulated standard now enjoys among creditor nations also would abate.

VII

The Goal of Monetary Policy

1.   Liberalism and the Gold Standard

Monetary policy of the preliberal era was either crude coin debasement, for the benefit of financial administration (only rarely intended as *Seisachtheia*,[1] i.e., to nullify outstanding debts), or still more crude paper money inflation. However, in addition to, sometimes even instead of, its fiscal goal, the driving motive behind paper money inflation very soon became the desire to favor the debtor at the expense of the creditor.

In opposing the depreciated paper standard, liberalism frequently took the position that after an inflation the value of paper money should be raised, through contraction, to its former parity with metallic money. It was only when men had learned that such a policy could not undo or reverse the "unfair" changes in wealth and income brought about by the previous inflationary period and that an increase in the purchasing power per unit [by contraction or deflation] also brings other unwanted shifts of wealth and income, that the demand for return to a metallic standard at the debased monetary unit's *current* parity gradually replaced the demand for restoration at the *old* parity.

In opposing a single precious metal standard, monetary policy exhausted itself in the fruitless attempt to make bimetallism an actuality. The results which must follow the establishment of a legal exchange ratio between the two precious metals, gold and silver, have long been known, even before Classical economics developed an understanding of the regularity of market phenomena. Again and again Gresham's

1. [According to Mises, *Seisachtheia* (Greek) was a term used in the seventh century B. C. to mean "shaking off of burdens." It described measures enacted to cancel in full or in part public and private debts; creditors then had to bear any loss, except to the extent that they might be indemnified by the government.—Ed.]

Law, which applied the general theory of price controls to the special case of money, demonstrated its validity. Eventually, efforts were abandoned to reach the ideal of a bimetallic standard. The next goal then became to free international trade, which was growing more and more important, from the effects of fluctuations in the ratio between the prices of the gold standard and the suppression of the alternating [bimetallic] and silver standards. Gold then became the world's money.

With the attainment of gold monometallism, liberals believed the goal of monetary policy had been reached. (The fact that they considered it necessary to supplement monetary policy through banking policy will be examined later in considerable detail.) The value of gold was then independent of any *direct* manipulation by governments, political policies, public opinion or parliaments. So long as the gold standard was maintained, there was no need to fear severe price disturbances from the side of money. The adherents of the gold standard wanted no more than this, even though it was not clear to them at first that this was all that *could* be attained.

2.   "Pure" Gold Standard Disregarded

We have seen how the purchasing power of gold has continuously declined since the turn of the century. That was not, as frequently maintained, simply the consequence of increased gold production. There is no way to know whether the increased production of gold would have been sufficient to satisfy the increased demand for money without increasing its purchasing power, if monetary policy had not intervened as it did. The gold exchange and flexible standards were adopted in a number of countries, not the "pure" gold standard as its advocates had expected. "Pure" gold standard countries embraced measures which were thought to be, and actually were, steps toward the exchange standard. Finally, since 1914, gold has been withdrawn from actual circulation almost everywhere. It is primarily due to these measures that gold declined in value, thus generating the current debate on monetary policy.

The fault found with the gold standard today is not, therefore, due to the gold standard itself. Rather, it is the result of a policy which deliberately seeks to undermine the gold standard in order to lower the costs of using money and especially to obtain "cheap money," i.e., lower interest rates for loans. Obviously, this policy cannot attain the goal it sets for itself. It must eventually bring not low interest on loans but rather price increases and distortion of economic development. In view of this, then, isn't it simply enough to abandon all attempts to use tricks of banking and monetary policy to lower interest rates, to reduce the costs of using and circulating money and to satisfy "needs" by promoting paper inflation?

The "pure" gold standard formed the foundation of the monetary system in the most important countries of Europe and America, as well as in Australia. This system remained in force until the outbreak of the World War [1914]. In the literature on the subject, it was also considered the ideal monetary policy until very recently. Yet the champions of this "pure" gold standard undoubtedly paid too little attention to changes in the purchasing power of monetary gold originating on the side of money. They scarcely noted the problem of the "stabilization" of the purchasing power of money, very likely considering it completely impractical. Today we may pride ourselves on having grasped the basic questions of price and monetary theory more thoroughly and on having discarded many of the concepts which dominated works on monetary policy of the recent past. However, precisely because we believe we have a better understanding of the problem of value today, we can no longer consider acceptable the proposals to construct a monetary system based on index numbers.

3.   The Index Standard

It is characteristic of current political thinking to welcome every suggestion which aims at enlarging the influence of government. If the Fisher and Keynes proposals[2] are approved on the grounds that they are intended to use government to make the formation of monetary value directly subservient to certain economic and political ends, this is understandable. However, anyone who approves of the index standard because he wants to see purchasing power "stabilized" will find himself in serious error.

Abandoning the pursuit of the chimera of a money of unchanging purchasing power calls for neither resignation nor disregard of the so-

2. [See above, p. 61, n. 3—Ed.]

cial consequences of changes in monetary value. The necessary conclusion from this discussion is that stability of the purchasing power of the monetary unit presumes stability of all exchange relationships and, therefore, the absolute abandonment of the market economy.

The question has been raised again and again: What will happen if, as a result of a technological revolution, gold production should increase to such an extent as to make further adherence to the gold standard impossible? A changeover to the index standard *must* follow then, it is asserted, so that it would only be expedient to make this change voluntarily now. However, it is futile to deal with monetary problems today which may or may not arise in the future. We do not know under what conditions steps will have to be taken toward solving them. It could be that, under certain circumstances, the solution may be to adopt a system based on an index number. However, this would appear doubtful. Even so, an index standard would hardly be a more suitable monetary standard than the one we now have. In spite of all its defects, the gold standard is a useful and not inexpedient standard.

PART II

Cyclical Policy to Eliminate Economic Fluctuations

Stabilization of the Purchasing Power of the Monetary Unit and Elimination of the Trade Cycle

1.   Currency School's Contribution

"Stabilization" of the purchasing power of the monetary unit would also lead, at the same time, to the ideal of an economy without any changes. In the stationary economy there would be no "ups" and "downs" of business. Then, the sequence of events would flow smoothly and steadily. Then, no unforeseen event would interrupt the provisioning of goods. Then, the acting individual would experience no disillusionment because events did not develop as he had assumed in planning his affairs to meet future demands.

First, we have seen that this ideal cannot be realized. Secondly, we have seen that this ideal is generally proposed as a goal only because the problems involved in the formation of purchasing power have not been thought through completely. Finally, we have seen that even if a stationary economy *could* actually be realized, it would certainly not accomplish what had been expected. Yet neither these facts nor the limiting of monetary policy to the maintenance of a "pure" gold standard means that the political slogan, "Eliminate the business cycle," is without value.

It is true that some authors who dealt with these problems had a rather vague idea that the "stabilization of the price level" was the way to attain the goals they set for cyclical policy. Yet cyclical policy was not completely spent on fruitless attempts to fix the purchasing power of money. Witness the fact that steps were undertaken to curb the boom through banking policy, and thus to prevent the decline, which inevitably follows the upswing, from going as far as it would if matters were allowed to run their course. These efforts—undertaken with enthusiasm at a time when people did not realize that anything like stabilization of monetary value would ever be conceived of and sought after—led to measures that had far-reaching consequences.

We should not forget for a moment the contribution which the Currency School made to the clarification of our problem. Not only did it contribute theoretically and scientifically but it contributed also to practical policy. The recent theoretical treatment of the problem—in the study of events and statistical data and in politics—rests entirely on the accomplishments of the Currency School. We have not surpassed Lord Overstone[1] so far as to be justified in disparaging his achievement.

Many modern students of cyclical movements are contemptuous of theory—not only of this or that theory but of *all* theories—and profess to let the facts speak for themselves. The delusion that theory must be distilled from the results of an impartial investigation of facts is more popular in cyclical theory than in any other field of economics. Yet, nowhere else is it clearer that there can be no understanding of the facts without theory.

Certainly it is no longer necessary to expose once more the errors in logic of the Historical-Empirical-Realistic approach to the "social sciences." Only recently has this task been most thoroughly undertaken once more by competent scholars. Nevertheless, we continually encounter attempts to deal with the business cycle problem while presumably rejecting theory.

In taking this approach one falls prey to a delusion which is incomprehensible. It is assumed that data on economic fluctuations are given clearly, directly and in a way that cannot be disputed. Thus it remains for science merely to interpret these fluctuations—and for the art of politics simply to find ways and means to eliminate them.

2.   Early Trade Cycle Theories

All business establishments do well at times and badly at others. There are times when the entrepreneur sees his profits increase daily more than he had anticipated and when, emboldened by these "windfalls," he proceeds to expand his operations. Then, due to an abrupt change

---

1. [Lord Samuel Jones Loyd Overstone (1796–1883), an early opponent of inconvertible paper money and a leading proponent of the principles of Peel's Act of 1844 limiting the use of banknotes, intended to eliminate business cycles.—Ed.]

in conditions, severe disillusionment follows this upswing, serious losses materialize, long established firms collapse, until widespread pessimism sets in which may frequently last for years. Such were the experiences which had already been forced on the attention of the businessman in capitalistic economies, long before discussions of the crisis problem began to appear in the literature. The sudden turn from the very sharp rise in prosperity—at least what appeared to be prosperity—to a very severe drop in profit opportunities was too conspicuous not to attract general attention. Even those who wanted to have nothing to do with the business world's "worship of filthy lucre" could not ignore the fact that people who were, or had been considered, rich yesterday were suddenly reduced to poverty, that factories were shut down, that construction projects were left uncompleted, and that workers could not find work. Naturally, nothing concerned the businessman more intimately than this very problem.

If an entrepreneur is asked what is going on here—leaving aside changes in the prices of individual commodities due to recognizable causes—he may very well reply that at times the entire "price level" tends upward and then at other times it tends downward. For inexplicable reasons, he would say, conditions arise under which it is impossible to dispose of all commodities, or almost all commodities, except at a loss. And what is most curious is that these depressing times always come when least expected, just when all business had been improving for some time so that people finally believed that a new age of steady and rapid progress was emerging.

Eventually, it must have become obvious to the more keenly thinking businessman that the genesis of the crisis should be sought in the preceding boom. The scientific investigator, whose view is naturally focused on the longer period, soon realized that economic upswings and downturns alternated with seeming regularity. Once this was established, the problem was halfway exposed and scientists began to ask questions as to how this apparent regularity might be explained and understood.

Theoretical analysis was able to reject, as completely false, two attempts to explain the crisis—the theories of general overproduction and of underconsumption. These two doctrines have disappeared from serious scientific discussion. They persist today only outside the realm of science—the theory of general overproduction, among the ideas held by the average citizen; and the underconsumption theory, in Marxist literature.

It was not so easy to criticize a third group of attempted explanations, those which sought to trace economic fluctuations back to periodical changes in natural phenomena affecting agricultural production. These doctrines cannot be reached by theoretical inquiry alone. Conceivably such events may occur and reoccur at regular intervals. Whether this actually is the case can be shown only by attempts to verify the theory through observation. So far, however, none of these "weather theories"[2] has successfully passed this test.

A whole series of a very different sort of attempts to explain the crisis are based on a definite irregularity in the psychological and intellectual talents of people. This irregularity is expressed in the economy by a change from confidence over the future, which inspires the boom, to despondency, which leads to the crisis and to stagnation of business. Or else this irregularity appears as a shift from boldly striking out in new directions to quietly following along already well-worn paths.

What should be pointed out about these doctrines and about the many other similar theories based on psychological variations is, first of all, that they do not explain. They merely pose the problem in a different way. They are not able to trace the change in business conditions back to a previously established and identified phenomenon. From the periodical fluctuations in psychological and intellectual data alone, without any further observation concerning the field of labor in the social or other sciences, we learn that such economic shifts as these may also be conceived of in a different way. So long as the course of such changes appears plausible only because of economic fluctuations between boom and bust, psychological and other related theories of the crisis amount to no more than tracing one unknown factor back to something else equally unknown.

3. The Circulation Credit Theory

Of all the theories of the trade cycle, only one has achieved and retained the rank of a fully-developed economic doctrine. That is the theory advanced by the Currency School, the theory which traces the cause of changes in business conditions to the phenomenon of circula-

2. Regarding the theories of Wm. Stanley Jevons, Henry L. Moore and Wm. Beveridge, see Wesley Clair Mitchell's *Business Cycles*, New York: National Bureau of Economic Research, 1927, pp. 12ff.

tion credit. All other theories of the crisis, even when they try to differ in other respects from the line of reasoning adopted by the Currency School, return again and again to follow in its footsteps. Thus, our attention is constantly being directed to observations which seem to corroborate the Currency School's interpretation.

In fact, it may be said that the Circulation Credit Theory of the Trade Cycle[3] is now accepted by all writers in the field and that the other theories advanced today aim only at explaining why the volume of circulation credit granted by the banks varies from time to time. All attempts to study the course of business fluctuations empirically and statistically, as well as all efforts to influence the shape of changes in business conditions by political action, are based on the Circulation Credit Theory of the Trade Cycle.

To show that an investigation of business cycles is not dealing with an imaginary problem, it is necessary to formulate a cycle theory that recognizes a cyclical regularity of changes in business conditions. If we could not find a satisfactory theory of cyclical changes, then the question would remain as to whether or not each individual crisis arose from a special cause which we would have to track down first. Originally, economics approached the problem of the crisis by trying to trace all crises back to specific "visible" and "spectacular" causes such as war, cataclysms of nature, adjustments to new economic data—for example, changes in consumption and technology, or the discovery of easier and more favorable methods of production. Crises which could not be explained in this way became the specific "problem of the crisis."

Neither the fact that unexplained crises still recur again and again nor the fact that they are always preceded by a distinct boom period is sufficient to prove with certainty that the problem to be dealt with is a unique phenomenon originating from one specific cause. Recurrences do not appear at regular intervals. And it is not hard to believe that the more a crisis contrasts with conditions in the immediately preceding period, the more severe it is considered to be. It might be assumed, therefore, that there is no specific "problem of the crisis" at all, and that the still unexplained crises must be explained by various special causes somewhat like the "crisis" which central European agriculture has faced since the rise of competition from the tilling of richer soil

---

3. As mentioned above, the most commonly used name for this theory is the "Monetary Theory." For a number of reasons the designation "Circulation Credit Theory" is preferable.

in eastern Europe and overseas, or the "crisis" of the European cotton industry at the time of the American Civil War. What is true of the crisis can also be applied to the boom. Here again, instead of seeking a general boom theory we could look for special causes for each individual boom.

Neither the connection between boom and bust nor the cyclical change of business conditions is a fact that can be established independent of theory. Only theory, business cycle theory, permits us to detect the wavy outline of a cycle in the tangled confusion of events.[4]

4. If expressions such as cycle, wave, etc., are used in business cycle theory, they are merely illustrations to simplify the presentation. One cannot and should not expect more from a simile which, as such, must always fall short of reality.

II

Circulation Credit Theory

1. The Banking School Fallacy

If notes are issued by the banks, or if bank deposits subject to check or other claim are opened, in excess of the amount of money kept in the vaults as cover, the effect on prices is similar to that obtained by an increase in the quantity of money. Since these fiduciary media, as notes and bank deposits not backed by metal are called, render the service of money as safe and generally accepted, payable on demand monetary claims, they may be used as money in all transactions. On that account, they are genuine money substitutes. Since they are in excess of the given total quantity of money in the narrower sense, they represent an increase in the quantity of money in the broader sense.

The practical significance of these undisputed and indisputable conclusions in the formation of prices is denied by the Banking School with its contention that the issue of such fiduciary media is strictly limited by the demand for money in the economy. The Banking School doctrine maintains that if fiduciary media are issued by the banks only to discount short-term commodity bills, then no more would come into circulation than were "needed" to liquidate the transactions. According to this doctrine, bank management could exert no influence on the volume of the commodity transactions activated. Purchases and sales from which short-term commodity bills originate would, by this very transaction, already have brought into existence paper credit which can be used, through further negotiation, for the exchange of goods and services. If the bank discounts the bill and, let us say, issues notes against it, that is, according to the Banking School, a neutral transaction as far as the market is concerned. Nothing more is involved than replacing one instrument which is technically less suitable for circulation, the bill of exchange, with a more suitable one, the note. Thus, according to this School, the effect of the issue of notes need not be to increase the quantity of money in circulation. If the bill of exchange is retired at maturity, then notes would flow back to the bank and new notes could enter circulation again only when new commodity bills came into being once more as a result of new business.

The weak link in this well-known line of reasoning lies in the assertion that the volume of transactions completed, as sales and purchases from which commodity bills can derive, is independent of the behavior of the banks. If the banks discount at a lower, rather than at a higher, interest rate, then more loans are made. Enterprises which are unprofitable at 5%, and hence are not undertaken, may be profitable at 4%. Therefore, by lowering the interest rate they charge, banks can intensify the demand for credit. Then, by satisfying this demand, they can increase the quantity of fiduciary media in circulation. Once this is recognized, the Banking Theory's only argument, that prices are not influenced by the issue of fiduciary media, collapses.

One must be careful not to speak simply of the effects of credit in general on prices, but to specify clearly the effects of "increased credit" or "credit expansion." A sharp distinction must be made between (1) credit which a bank grants by lending its own funds or funds placed at its disposal by depositors, which we call "commodity credit," and (2) that which is granted by the creation of fiduciary media, i.e., notes and deposits not covered by money, which we call "circulation credit."[1] It is only through the granting of circulation credit that the prices of all commodities and services are directly affected.

If the banks grant circulation credit by discounting a three month bill of exchange, they exchange a future good—a claim payable in three months—for a present good that they produce out of nothing. It is not correct, therefore, to maintain that it is immaterial whether the bill of exchange is discounted by a bank of issue or whether it remains in circulation, passing from hand to hand. Whoever takes the bill of exchange in trade can do so only if he has the resources. But the bank of issue discounts by creating the necessary funds and putting them into circulation. To be sure, the fiduciary media flow back again to the bank at expiration of the note. If the bank does not give

---

1. [For further explanation of the distinction between "commodity credit" and "circulation credit" see mises's 1946 essay "The Trade Cycle and Credit Expansion," reprinted below, pp. 187ff., especially pp. 191–192.—Ed.]

the fiduciary media out again, precisely the same consequences appear as those which come from a decrease in the quantity of money in its broader sense.

2.   Early Effects of Credit Expansion

The fact that in the regular course of banking operations the banks issue fiduciary media only as loans to producers and merchants means that they are not used directly for purposes of consumption.[2] Rather, these fiduciary media are used first of all for production, that is to buy factors of production and pay wages. The first prices to rise, therefore, as a result of an increase of the quantity of money in the broader sense, caused by the issue of such fiduciary media, are those of raw materials, semi-manufactured products, other goods of higher orders, and wage rates. Only later do the prices of goods of the first order [consumers' goods] follow. Changes in the purchasing power of a monetary unit, brought about by the issue of fiduciary media, follow a different path and have different accompanying social side effects from those produced by a new discovery of precious metals or by the issue of paper money. Still in the last analysis, the effect on prices is similar in both instances.

Changes in the purchasing power of the monetary unit do not directly affect the height of the rate of interest. An indirect influence on the height of the interest rate can take place as a result of the fact that shifts in wealth and income relationships, appearing as a result of the change in the value of the monetary unit, influence savings and, thus, the accumulation of capital. If a depreciation of the monetary unit favors the wealthier members of society at the expense of the poorer, its effect will probably be an increase in capital accumulation since the well-to-do are the more important savers. The more they put aside, the more their incomes and fortunes will grow.

If monetary depreciation is brought about by an issue of fiduciary media, and if wage rates do not promptly follow the increase in commodity prices, then the decline in purchasing power will certainly make this effect much more severe. This is the "forced savings" which

2. [In 1928, when this paper was written, fiduciary media were issued only by discounting what Mises called commodity bills, or short-term ninety days or less) bills of exchange endorsed by a buyer and a seller and constituting a lien on the goods sold.—Ed.]

is quite properly stressed in recent literature.[3] However, three things should not be forgotten. First, it always depends upon the data of the particular case whether shifts of wealth and income, which lead to increased saving, are actually set in motion. Secondly, under circumstances which need not be discussed further here, by falsifying economic calculation, based on monetary bookkeeping calculations, a very substantial devaluation can lead to capital consumption (such a situation did take place temporarily during the recent inflationary period). Thirdly, as advocates of inflation through credit expansion should observe, any legislative measure which transfers resources to the "rich" at the expense of the "poor" will also foster capital formation.

Eventually, the issue of fiduciary media in such manner can also lead to increased capital accumulation within narrow limits and, hence, to a further reduction of the interest rate. In the beginning, however, an immediate and direct decrease in the loan rate appears with the issue of fiduciary media, but this immediate decrease in the loan rate is distinct in character and degree from the later reduction. The new funds offered on the money market by the banks must obviously bring pressure to bear on the rate of interest. The supply and demand for loan money were adjusted at the interest rate prevailing *before* the issue of any additional supply of fiduciary media. Additional loans can be placed only if the interest rate is lowered. Such loans are profitable for the banks because the increase in the supply of fiduciary media calls for no expenditure except for the mechanical costs of banking (i.e., printing the notes and bookkeeping). The banks can, therefore, undercut the interest rates which would otherwise appear on the loan market, in the absence of their intervention. Since competition from them compels other money lenders to lower *their* interest charges, the market interest rate must therefore decline. But can this reduction be maintained? *That* is the problem.

---

3. Albert Hahn and Joseph Schumpeter have given me credit for the expression "forced savings" or "compulsory savings." See Hahn's article on "Credit" in *Handwörterbuch der Staatswissenschaften* (4th ed., Vol. V, p. 951) and Schumpeter's *The Theory of Economic Development* (2nd German language ed., 1926; [English trans., Harvard Univ. Press, 1934, p. 109n.]). To be sure, I described the phenomenon in 1912 in the first German language edition of *The Theory of Money and Credit* [see English translation (Yale, 1953), pp. 208ff. and 347ff., (Liberty Fund, 1981), pp. 238ff., 368ff.]. However, I do not believe the expression itself was actually used there.

3.   Inevitable Effects of Credit Expansion on Interest Rates

In conformity with Wicksell's terminology, we shall use "natural interest rate" to describe that interest rate which would be established by supply and demand if real goods were loaned *in natura* [directly, as in barter] without the intermediary of money. "Money rate of interest" will be used for that interest rate asked on loans made in money or money substitutes. Through continued expansion of fiduciary media, it is possible for the banks to force the money rate down to the actual cost of the banking operations, practically speaking that is almost to zero. As a result, several authors have concluded that interest could be completely abolished in this way. Whole schools of reformers have wanted to use banking policy to make credit gratuitous and thus to solve the "social question." No reasoning person today, however, believes that interest can ever be abolished, nor doubts but what, if the "money interest rate" is depressed by the expansion of fiduciary media, it must sooner or later revert once again to the "natural interest rate." The question is only how this inevitable adjustment takes place. The answer to this will explain at the same time the fluctuations of the business cycle.

The Currency Theory limited the problem too much. It only considered the situation that was of practical significance for the England of its time—that is, when the issue of fiduciary media is increased in one country while remaining unchanged in others. Under these assumptions, the situation is quite clear: General price increases at home; hence an increase in imports, a drop in commodity exports; and with this, as notes can circulate only within the country, an outflow of metallic money. To obtain metallic money for export, holders of notes present them for redemption; the metallic reserves of the banks decline; and consideration for their own solvency then forces them to restrict the credit offered.

That is the instant at which the business upswing, brought about by the availability of easy credit, is demonstrated to be illusory prosperity. An abrupt reaction sets in. The "money rate of interest" shoots up; enterprises from which credit is withdrawn collapse and sweep along with them the banks which are their creditors. A long persisting period of business stagnation now follows. The banks, warned by this experience into observing restraint, not only no longer underbid the "natural interest rate" but exercise extreme caution in granting credit.

4.   The Price Premium

In order to complete this interpretation, we must, first of all, consider the price premium. As the banks start to expand the circulation credit, the anticipated upward movement of prices results in the appearance of a positive price premium. Even if the banks do not lower the actual interest rate any more, the gap widens between the "money interest rate" and the "natural interest rate" which would prevail in the absence of their intervention. Since loan money is now cheaper to acquire than circumstances warrant, entrepreneurial ambitions expand.

New businesses are started in the expectation that the necessary capital can be secured by obtaining credit. To be sure, in the face of growing demand, the banks now raise the "money interest rate." Still they do not discontinue granting further credit. They expand the supply of fiduciary media issued, with the result that the purchasing power of the monetary unit must decline still further. Certainly the actual "money interest rate" increases during the boom, but it continues to lag behind the rate which would conform to the market, i.e., the "natural interest rate" augmented by the positive price premium.

So long as this situation prevails, the upswing continues. Inventories of goods are readily sold. Prices and profits rise. Business enterprises are overwhelmed with orders because everyone anticipates further price increases and workers find employment at increasing wage rates. However, this situation cannot last forever!

5.   Malinvestment of Available Capital Goods

The "natural interest rate" is established at that height which tends toward equilibrium on the market. The tendency is toward a condition where no capital goods are idle, no opportunities for starting profitable enterprises remain unexploited and the only projects not undertaken are those which no longer yield a profit at the prevailing "natural interest rate." Assume, however, that the equilibrium, toward which the market is moving, is disturbed by the interference of the banks. Money may be obtained below the "natural interest rate." As a result businesses may be started which weren't profitable before, and which become profitable only through the lower than "natural interest rate" which appears with the expansion of circulation credit.

Here again, we see the difference which exists between a drop in purchasing power, caused by the expansion of circulation credit, and a loss of purchasing power, brought about by an increase in the quantity of money. In the latter case [i.e., with an increase in the quantity of money in the narrower sense] the prices first affected are either (1) those of consumers' goods only or (2) the prices of both consumers' *and* producers' goods. Which it will be depends on whether those first receiving the new quantities of money use this new wealth for consumption or production. However, if the decrease in purchasing power is caused by an increase in bank created fiduciary media, then it is the prices of producers' goods which are first affected. The prices of consumers' goods follow only to the extent that wages and profits rise.

Since it always requires some time for the market to reach full "equilibrium," the "static" or "natural"[4] prices, wage rates and interest rates never actually appear. The process leading to their establishment is never completed before changes occur which once again indicate a new "equilibrium." At times, even on the unhampered market, there are some unemployed workers, unsold consumers' goods and quantities of unused factors of production, which would not exist under "static equilibrium." With the revival of business and productive activity, these reserves are in demand right away. However, once they are gone, the increase in the supply of fiduciary media necessarily leads to disturbances of a special kind.

In a given economic situation, the opportunities for production, which may actually be carried out, are limited by the supply of capital goods available. Roundabout methods of production can be adopted only so far as the means for subsistence exist to maintain the workers during the entire period of the expanded process. All those projects, for the completion of which means are not available, must be left uncompleted, even though they may appear technically feasible—that is, if one disregards the supply of capital. However, such businesses, because of the lower loan rate offered by the banks, appear for the moment to be profitable and are, therefore, initiated. However, the existing resources are insufficient. Sooner or later this must become evident. Then it will become apparent that production has gone astray, that plans were drawn up in excess of the economic means available, that speculation, i.e., activity aimed at the provision of future goods, was misdirected.

4. In the language of Knut Wicksell and the Classical economists.

6.   "Forced Savings"

In recent years, considerable significance has been attributed to the fact that "forced savings," which may appear as a result of the drop in purchasing power that follows an increase of fiduciary media, lead to an increase in the supply of capital. The subsistence fund is made to go farther, due to the fact that (1) the workers consume less because wage rates tend to lag behind the rise in the prices of commodities, and (2) those who reap the advantage of this reduction in the workers' incomes save at least a part of their gain. Whether "forced savings" actually appear depends, as noted above, on the circumstances in each case. There is no need to go into this any further.

Nevertheless, establishing the existence of "forced savings" does not mean that bank expansion of circulation credit does not lead to the initiation of more roundabout production than available capabilities would warrant. To prove that, one must be able to show that the banks are only in a position to depress the "money interest rate" and expand the issue of fiduciary media to the extent that the "natural interest rate" declines as a result of "forced savings." This assumption is simply absurd and there is no point in arguing it further. It is almost inconceivable that anyone should want to maintain it.

What concerns us is the problem brought about by the banks, in reducing the "money rate of interest" *below* the "natural rate." For our problem, it is immaterial how much the "natural interest rate" may also decline under certain circumstances and within narrow limits, as a result of this action by the banks. No one doubts that "forced savings" can reduce the "natural interest rate" only fractionally, as compared with the reduction in the "money interest rate" which produces the "forced savings."[5]

The resources which are claimed for the newly initiated longer time consuming methods of production are unavailable for those processes where they would otherwise have been put to use. The reduction in the loan rate benefits all producers, so that all producers are now in a position to pay higher wage rates and higher prices for the material factors of production. Their competition drives up wage rates and the prices of

---

5. I believe this should be pointed out here again, although I have exhausted everything to be said on the subject [see above pp. 107–108] and in *The Theory of Money and Credit* [(Yale, 1953), pp. 361ff.; (Liberty Fund, 1981), pp. 400ff.]. Anyone who has followed the discussions of recent years will realize how important it is to stress these things again and again.

the other factors of production. Still, except for the possibilities already discussed, this does not increase the size of the labor force or the supply of available goods of the higher order. The means of subsistence are not sufficient to provide for the workers during the extended period of production. It becomes apparent that the proposal for the new, longer, roundabout production was not adjusted with a view to the actual capital situation. For one thing, the enterprises realize that the resources available to them are not sufficient to continue their operations. They find that "money" is scarce.

That is precisely what has happened. The general increase in prices means that all businesses need more funds than had been anticipated at their "launching." More resources are required to complete them. However, the increased quantity of fiduciary media loaned out by the banks is already exhausted. The banks can no longer make additional loans at the same interest rates. As a result, they must raise the loan rate once more for two reasons. In the first place, the appearance of the positive price premium forces them to pay higher interest for outside funds which they borrow. Then also, they must discriminate among the many applicants for credit. Not all enterprises can afford this increased interest rate. Those which cannot run into difficulties.

7.   A Habit-forming Policy

Now, in extending circulation credit, the banks do not proceed by pumping a limited dosage of new fiduciary media into circulation and then stop. They expand the fiduciary media continuously for some time, sending, so to speak, after the first offering, a second, third, fourth, and so on. They do not simply undercut the "natural interest rate" once, and then adjust promptly to the new situation. Instead they continue the practice of making loans below the "natural interest rate" for some time. To be sure, the increasing volume of demands on them for credit may cause them to raise the "money rate of interest." Yet, even if the banks revert to the former "natural rate," the rate which prevailed before their credit expansion affected the market, they still lag behind the rate which would now exist on the market if they were not continuing to expand credit. This is because a positive price premium must now be included in the new "natural rate." With the help of this new quantity of fiduciary media, the banks now take care of the businessmen's intensified demand for credit. Thus, the crisis does not appear yet. The enterprises using more roundabout methods of production, which have been started, are continued. Because prices rise still further, the earlier calculations of the entrepreneurs are realized. They make profits. In short, the boom continues.

8.   The Inevitable Crisis and Cycle

The crisis breaks out only when the banks alter their conduct to the extent that they discontinue issuing any more new fiduciary media and stop undercutting the "natural interest rate." They may even take steps to restrict circulation credit. *When* they actually do this, and *why*, is still to be examined. First of all, however, we must ask ourselves whether it is possible for the banks to stay on the course upon which they have embarked, permitting new quantities of fiduciary media to flow into circulation continuously and proceeding always to make loans below the rate of interest which would prevail on the market in the absence of their interference with newly created fiduciary media.

If the banks could proceed in this manner, with businesses improving continually, could they then provide for lasting good times? Would they then be able to make the boom eternal?

They cannot do this. The reason they cannot is that inflationism carried on *ad infinitum* is not a workable policy. If the issue of fiduciary media is expanded continuously, prices rise ever higher and at the same time the positive price premium also rises. (We shall disregard the fact that consideration for (1) the continually declining monetary reserves relative to fiduciary media and (2) the banks' operating costs must sooner or later compel them to discontinue the further expansion of circulation credit.) It is precisely because, and only because, no end to the prolonged "flood" of expanding fiduciary media is foreseen that it leads to still sharper price increases and, finally, to a panic in which prices and the loan rate move erratically upward.

Suppose the banks still did not want to give up the race? Suppose, in order to depress the loan rate, they wanted to satisfy the continuously expanding desire for credit by issuing still more circulation credit? Then they would only hasten the end, the collapse of the entire system of fiduciary media. The inflation can continue only so long as the conviction persists that it will one day cease. Once people are persuaded that the inflation will *not* stop, they turn from the use of this money. They flee then to "real values," foreign money, the precious metals, and barter.

Sooner or later, the crisis *must* inevitably break out as the result of a change in the conduct of the banks. The later the crack-up comes, the longer the period in which the calculation of the entrepreneurs is misguided by the issue of additional fiduciary media. The greater this additional quantity of fiduciary money, the more factors of production have been firmly committed in the form of investments which appeared profitable only because of the artificially reduced interest rate and which prove to be unprofitable now that the interest rate has again been raised. Great losses are sustained as a result of misdirected capital investments. Many new structures remain unfinished. Others, already completed, close down operations. Still others are carried on because, after writing off losses which represent a waste of capital, operation of the existing structure pays at least something.

The crisis, with its unique characteristics, is followed by stagnation. The misguided enterprises and businesses of the boom period are already liquidated. Bankruptcy and adjustment have cleared up the situation. The banks have become cautious. They fight shy of expanding circulation credit. They are not inclined to give an ear to credit applications from schemers and promoters. Not only is the artificial stimulus to business, through the expansion of circulation credit, lacking, but even businesses which *would* be feasible, considering the capital goods available, are not attempted because the general feeling of discouragement makes every innovation appear doubtful. Prevailing "money interest rates" fall *below* the "natural interest rates."

When the crisis breaks out, loan rates bound sharply upward because threatened enterprises offer extremely high interest rates for the funds to acquire the resources, with the help of which they hope to save themselves. Later, as the panic subsides, a situation develops, as a result of the restriction of circulation credit and attempts to dispose of large inventories, causing prices [and the "money interest rate"] to fall steadily and leading to the appearance of a negative price premium. This reduced rate of loan interest is adhered to for some time, even after the decline in prices comes to a standstill, when a negative price premium no longer corresponds to conditions. Thus, it comes about that the "money interest rate" is lower than the "natural rate." Yet, because the unfortunate experiences of the recent crisis have made everyone uneasy, the incentive to business activity is not as strong as circumstances would otherwise warrant. Quite a time passes before capital funds, increased once again by savings accumulated in the meantime, exert sufficient pressure on the loan interest rate for an expansion of entrepreneurial activity to resume. With this development, the low point is passed and the new boom begins.

III

The Reappearance of Cycles

1.　Metallic Standard Fluctuations

From the instant when the banks start expanding the volume of circulation credit until the moment they stop such behavior, the course of events is substantially similar to that provoked by any increase in the quantity of money. The difference results from the fact that fiduciary media generally come into circulation through the banks, i.e., as loans, while increases in the quantity of money appear as additions to the wealth and income of specific individuals. This has already been mentioned and will not be further considered here. Considerably more significant for us is another distinction between the two.

Such increases and decreases in the quantity of money have no connection with increases or decreases in the demand for money. If the demand for money grows in the wake of a population increase or a progressive reduction of barter and self-sufficiency resulting in increased monetary transactions, there is absolutely no need to increase the quantity of money. It might even decrease. In any event, it would be most extraordinary if changes in the demand for money were balanced by reciprocal changes in its quantity so that both changes were concealed and no change took place in the monetary unit's purchasing power.

Changes in the value of the monetary unit are always taking place in the economy. Periods of declining purchasing power alternate with those of increasing purchasing power. Under a metallic standard, these changes are usually so slow and so insignificant that their effect is not at all violent. Nevertheless, we must recognize that even under a precious metal standard periods of ups and downs would still alternate at irregular intervals. In addition to the standard metallic money, such a standard would recognize only token coins for petty transactions.

There would, of course, be no paper money or any other currency (i.e., either notes or bank accounts subject to check which are not fully covered). Yet even then, one would be able to speak of economic "ups," "downs" and "waves." However, one would hardly be inclined to refer to such minor alternating "ups" and "downs" as regularly recurring cycles. During these periods when purchasing power moved in one direction, whether up or down, it would probably move so slightly that businessmen would scarcely notice the changes. Only economic historians would become aware of them. Moreover, the fact is that the transition from a period of rising prices to one of falling prices would be so slight that neither panic nor crisis would appear. This would also mean that businessmen and news reports of market activities would be less occupied with the "long waves" of the trade cycle.[1]

2. Infrequent Recurrences of Paper Money Inflations

The effects of inflations brought about by increases in paper money are quite different. They also produce price increases and hence "good business conditions," which are further intensified by the apparent encouragement of exports and the hampering of imports. Once the inflation comes to an end, whether by a providential halt to further increases in the quantity of money (as for instance recently in France and Italy) or through complete debasement of the paper money due to inflationary policy carried to its final conclusions (as in Germany in 1923), then the "stabilization crisis"[2] appears. The cause and appearance of this crisis correspond precisely to those of the crisis which comes at the close of a period of circulation credit expansion. One must clearly distinguish *this* crisis [i.e., when increases in the quantity of money are simply halted] from the consequences which must result when the cessation of inflation is followed by deflation.

There is no regularity as to the recurrence of paper money infla-

1. To avoid misunderstanding, it should be pointed out that the expression "long waves" of the trade cycle is not to be understood here as it was used by either Wilhelm Röpke or N. D. Kondratieff. Röpke (*Die Konjunktur*, Jena, 1922, p. 21) considered "long-wave cycles" to be those which lasted five to ten years generally. Kondratieff ("Die langen Wellen der Konjunktur" in *Archiv für Sozialwissenschaft*, Vol. 56, pp. 573ff.) tried to prove, unsuccessfully in my judgment, that, in addition to the seven to eleven year cycles of business conditions which he called medium cycles, there were also regular cyclical waves averaging fifty years in length.

2. [The German term, "Sanierungskrise," means literally "restoration crisis," i.e., the crisis which comes at the shift to more "healthy" monetary relationships.—Ed.]

tions. They generally originate in a certain political attitude, not from events within the economy itself. One can only say, with certainty, that after a country has pursued an inflationist policy to its end or, at least, to substantial lengths, it cannot soon use this means again successfully to serve its financial interests. The people, as a result of their experience, will have become distrustful and would resist any attempt at a renewal of inflation.

Even at the very beginning of a new inflation, people would reject the notes or accept them only at a far greater discount than the actual increased quantity would otherwise warrant. As a rule, such an unusually high discount is characteristic of the final phases of an inflation. Thus an early attempt to return to a policy of paper money inflation must either fail entirely or come very quickly to a catastrophic conclusion. One can assume—and monetary history confirms this, or at least does not contradict it—that a new generation must grow up before consideration can again be given to bolstering the government's finances with the printing press.

Many states have never pursued a policy of paper money inflation. Many have resorted to it only once in their history. Even the states traditionally known for their printing press money have not repeated the experiment often. Austria waited almost a generation after the banknote inflation of the Napoleonic era before embarking on an inflation policy again. Even then, the inflation was in more modest proportions than at the beginning of the nineteenth century. Almost a half century passed between the end of her second and the beginning of her third and most recent period of inflation. It is by no means possible to speak of cyclical reappearances of paper money inflations.

3.   The Cyclical Process of Credit Expansions

Regularity can be detected only with respect to the phenomena originating out of circulation credit. Crises have reappeared every few years since banks issuing fiduciary media began to play an important role in the economic life of people. Stagnation followed crisis, and following these came the boom again. More than ninety years ago Lord Overstone described the sequence in a remarkably graphic manner:

> We find it [the "state of trade"] subject to various conditions which are periodically returning; it revolves apparently in an established cycle.

> First we find it in a state of quiescence,—next improvement,—growing
> confidence,—prosperity,—excitement,—overtrading,—convulsion,—
> pressure,—stagnation,—distress,—ending again in quiescence.[3]

This description, unrivaled for its brevity and clarity, must be kept in mind to realize how wrong it is to give later economists credit for transforming the problem of the crisis into the problem of general business conditions.

Attempts have been made, with little success, to supplement the observation that business cycles recur by attributing a definite time period to the sequence of events. Theories which sought the source of economic change in recurring cosmic events have, as might be expected, leaned in this direction. A study of economic history fails to support such assumptions. It shows recurring ups and downs in business conditions, but not ups and downs of equal length.

The problem to be solved is the recurrence of fluctuations in business activity. The Circulation Credit Theory shows us, in rough outline, the typical course of a cycle. However, so far as we have as yet analyzed the theory, it still does not explain why the cycle always recurs.

According to the Circulation Credit Theory, it is clear that the direct stimulus which provokes the fluctuations is to be sought in the conduct of the banks. Insofar as they start to reduce the "money rate of interest" below the "natural rate of interest," they expand circulation credit, and thus divert the course of events away from the path of normal development. They bring about changes in relationships which must necessarily lead to boom and crisis. Thus, the problem consists of asking what leads the banks again and again to renew attempts to expand the volume of circulation credit.

Many authors believe that the instigation of the banks' behavior comes from outside, that certain events induce them to pump more fiduciary media into circulation and that they would behave differently if these circumstances failed to appear. I was also inclined to this view in the first edition of my book on monetary theory.[4] I could not un-

---

3. Overstone, Samuel Jones Loyd (Lord). "Reflections Suggested by a Perusal of Mr. J. Horsley Palmer's Pamphlet on the Causes and Consequences of the Pressure on the Money Market," 1837. (Reprinted in *Tracts and Other Publications on Metallic and Paper Currency*, London, 1857), p. 31.

4. See *Theorie des Geldes und der Umlaufsmittel* (1912), pp. 433ff. I had been deeply impressed by the fact that Lord Overstone was also apparently inclined to this interpretation. See his *Reflections*, pp. 32ff. [These paragraphs were not included in the second German edition (1924) from which the English translation, *The Theory of Money and Credit*, was made.—Ed.]

derstand why the banks didn't learn from experience. I thought they would certainly persist in a policy of caution and restraint, if they were not led by outside circumstances to abandon it. Only later did I become convinced that it was useless to look to an outside stimulus for the change in the conduct of the banks. Only later did I also become convinced that fluctuations in general business conditions were completely dependent on the relationship of the quantity of fiduciary media in circulation to demand.

Each new issue of fiduciary media has the consequences described above. First of all, it depresses the loan rate and then it reduces the monetary unit's purchasing power. Every subsequent issue brings the same result. The establishment of new banks of issue and their step-by-step expansion of circulation credit provides the means for a business boom and, as a result, leads to the crisis with its accompanying decline. We can readily understand that the banks issuing fiduciary media, in order to improve their chances for profit, may be ready to expand the volume of credit granted and the number of notes issued. What calls for special explanation is why attempts are made again and again to improve general economic conditions by the expansion of circulation credit in spite of the spectacular failure of such efforts in the past.

The answer must run as follows: According to the prevailing ideology of businessman and economist-politician, the reduction of the interest rate is considered an essential goal of economic policy. Moreover, the expansion of circulation credit is assumed to be the appropriate means to achieve this goal.

4.   The Mania for Lower Interest Rates

The naive inflationist theory of the seventeenth and eighteenth centuries could not stand up in the long run against the criticism of economics. In the nineteenth century, that doctrine was held only by obscure authors who had no connection with scientific inquiry or practical economic policy. For purely political reasons, the school of empirical and historical "Realism" did not pay attention to problems of economic theory. It was due only to this neglect of theory that the naive theory of inflation was once more able to gain prestige temporarily during the World War, especially in Germany.

The doctrine of inflationism by way of fiduciary media was more durable. Adam Smith had battered it severely, as had others even before him, especially the American William Douglass.[5] Many, notably in the Currency School, had followed. But then came a reversal. The Banking School confused the situation. Its founders failed to see the error in their doctrine. They failed to see that the expansion of circulation credit lowered the interest rate. They even argued that it was impossible to expand credit beyond the "needs of business." So there are seeds in the Banking Theory which need only to be developed to reach the conclusion that the interest rate can be reduced by the conduct of the banks. At the very least, it must be admitted that those who dealt with those problems did not sufficiently understand the reasons for opposing credit expansion to be able to overcome the public clamor for the banks to provide "cheap money."

In discussions of the rate of interest, the economic press adopted the questionable jargon of the business world, speaking of a "scarcity" or an "abundance" of money and calling the short-term loan market the "money market." Banks issuing fiduciary media, warned by experience to be cautious, practiced discretion and hesitated to indulge the universal desire of the press, political parties, parliaments, governments, entrepreneurs, landowners and workers for cheaper credit. Their reluctance to expand credit was falsely attributed to reprehensible motives. Even newspapers, that knew better, and politicians, who should have known better, never tired of asserting that the banks of issue could certainly discount larger sums more cheaply if they were not trying to hold the interest rate as high as possible out of concern for their own profitability and the interests of their controlling capitalists.

Almost without exception, the great European banks of issue on the continent were established with the expectation that the loan rate could be reduced by issuing fiduciary media. Under the influence of the Currency School doctrine, at first in England and then in other countries where old laws did not restrict the issue of notes, arrangements were made to limit the expansion of circulation credit, at least of that part granted through the issue of uncovered banknotes. Still, the Currency Theory lost out as a result of criticism by Tooke (1774–1858) and his followers. Although it was considered risky to abolish the laws which restricted the issue of notes, no harm was seen in circumventing them. Actually, the letter of the banking laws provided for a concen-

5. [William Douglass (1691–1752), a physician, came to America in 1716. His "A Discourse Concerning the Currencies of the British Plantations in America" (1739) first appeared anonymously.—Ed.]

tration of the nation's supply of precious metals in the vaults of banks of issue. This permitted an increase in the issue of fiduciary media and played an important role in the expansion of the gold exchange standard.

Before the war [1914], there was no hesitation in Germany in openly advocating withdrawal of gold from trade so that the Reichsbank might issue sixty marks in notes for every twenty marks in gold added to its stock. Propaganda was also made for expanding the use of payments by check with the explanation that this was a means to lower the interest rate substantially.[6] The situation was similar elsewhere, although perhaps more cautiously expressed.

Every single fluctuation in general business conditions—the upswing to the peak of the wave and the decline into the trough which follows—is prompted by the attempt of the banks of issue to reduce the loan rate and thus expand the volume of circulation credit through an increase in the supply of fiduciary media (i.e., banknotes and checking accounts not fully backed by money). The fact that these efforts are resumed again and again in spite of their widely deplored consequences, causing one business cycle after another, can be attributed to the predominance of an ideology—an ideology which regards rising commodity prices and especially a low rate of interest as goals of economic policy. The theory is that even this second goal may be attained by the expansion of fiduciary media. Both crisis and depression are lamented. Yet, because the causal connection between the behavior of the banks of issue and the evils complained about is not correctly interpreted, a policy with respect to interest is advocated which, in the last analysis, must necessarily always lead to crisis and depression.

5. Free Banking

Every deviation from the prices, wage rates and interest rates which would prevail on the unhampered market must lead to disturbances of the economic "equilibrium." This disturbance, brought about by attempts to depress the interest rate artificially, is precisely the cause of the crisis.

6. See the examples cited in *The Theory of Money and Credit* [(Yalé, 1953), pp. 387–390; (Liberty Fund, 1981), 426–429.—Ed.].

The ultimate cause, therefore, of the phenomenon of wave after wave of economic ups and downs is ideological in character. The cycles will not disappear so long as people believe that the rate of interest may be reduced, not through the accumulation of capital, but by banking policy.

Even if governments had never concerned themselves with the issue of fiduciary media, there would still be banks of issue and fiduciary media in the form of notes as well as checking accounts. There would then be no legal limitation on the issue of fiduciary media. Free banking would prevail. However, banks would have to be especially cautious because of the sensitivity to loss of reputation of their fiduciary media, which no one would be forced to accept. In the course of time, the inhabitants of capitalistic countries would learn to differentiate between good and bad banks. Those living in "undeveloped" countries would distrust all banks. No government would exert pressure on the banks to discount on easier terms than the banks themselves could justify. However, the managers of solvent and highly respected banks, the only banks whose fiduciary media would enjoy the general confidence essential for money-substitute quality, would have learned from past experiences. Even if they scarcely detected the deeper correlations, they would nevertheless know how far they might go without precipitating the danger of a breakdown.

The cautious policy of restraint on the part of respected and well-established banks would compel the more irresponsible managers of other banks to follow suit, however much they might want to discount more generously. For the expansion of circulation credit can never be the act of one individual bank alone, nor even of a group of individual banks. It always requires that the fiduciary media be *generally* accepted as a money substitute. If several banks of issue, each enjoying equal rights, existed side by side, and if some of them sought to expand the volume of circulation credit while the others did not alter their conduct, then at every bank clearing, demand balances would regularly appear in favor of the conservative enterprises. As a result of the presentation of notes for redemption and withdrawal of their cash balances, the expanding banks would very quickly be compelled once more to limit the scale of their emissions.

In the course of the development of a banking system with fiduciary media, crises could not have been avoided. However, as soon as bankers recognized the dangers of expanding circulation credit, they would

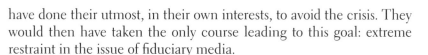

have done their utmost, in their own interests, to avoid the crisis. They would then have taken the only course leading to this goal: extreme restraint in the issue of fiduciary media.

6.   Government Intervention in Banking

The fact that the development of fiduciary media banking took a different turn may be attributed entirely to the circumstance that the issue of banknotes (which for a long time were the only form of fiduciary media and are today [1928] still the more important, even in the United States and England) became a public concern. The private bankers and joint-stock banks were supplanted by the politically privileged banks of issue because the governments favored the expansion of circulation credit for reasons of fiscal and credit policy. The privileged institutions could proceed unhesitatingly in the granting of credit, not only because they usually held a monopoly in the issue of notes, but also because they could rely on the government's help in an emergency. The private banker would go bankrupt if he ventured too far in the issue of credit. The privileged bank received permission to suspend payments and its notes were made legal tender at face value.

If the knowledge derived from the Currency Theory had led to the conclusion that fiduciary media should be deprived of all special privileges and placed, like other claims, under general law in every respect and without exception, this would probably have contributed more toward eliminating the threat of crises than was actually accomplished by establishing rigid proportions for the issue of fiduciary media in the form of notes and restricting the freedom of banks to issue fiduciary media in the form of checking accounts. The principle of free banking was limited to the field of checking accounts. In fact, it could not function here to bring about restraint on the part of banks and bankers. Public opinion decreed that government should be guided by a different policy—a policy of coming to the assistance of the central banks of issue in times of crises. To permit the Bank of England to lend a helping hand to banks which had gotten into trouble by expanding circulation credit, the Peel Act was suspended in 1847, 1857 and 1866. Such assistance, in one form or another, has been offered time and again everywhere.

In the United States, national banking legislation made it technically difficult, if not entirely impossible, to grant such aid. The system was considered especially unsatisfactory, precisely because of the legal obstacles it placed in the path of helping grantors of credit who became insolvent and of supporting the value of circulation credit they had granted. Among the reasons leading to the significant revision of the American banking system [i.e., the Federal Reserve Act of 1913], the most important was the belief that provisions must be made for times of crises. In other words, just as the emergency institution of Clearing House Certificates was able to save expanding banks, so should technical expedients be used to prevent the breakdown of the banks and bankers whose conduct had led to the crisis. It was usually considered especially important to shield the banks which expanded circulation credit from the consequences of their conduct. One of the chief tasks of the central banks of issue was to jump into this breach. It was also considered the duty of those other banks who, thanks to foresight, had succeeded in preserving their solvency, even in the general crisis, to help fellow banks in difficulty.

7.   Intervention No Remedy

It may well be asked whether the damage inflicted by misguiding entrepreneurial activity by artificially lowering the loan rate would be greater if the crisis were permitted to run its course. Certainly many saved by the intervention would be sacrificed in the panic, but if such enterprises were permitted to fail, others would prosper. Still the total loss brought about by the "boom" (which the crisis did not produce, but only made evident) is largely due to the fact that factors of production were expended for fixed investments which, in the light of economic conditions, were not the most urgent. As a result, these factors of production are now lacking for more urgent uses. If intervention prevents the transfer of goods from the hands of imprudent entrepreneurs to those who would now take over because they have evidenced better foresight, this imbalance becomes neither less significant nor less perceptible.

In any event, the practice of intervening for the benefit of banks rendered insolvent by the crisis, and of the customers of these banks, has resulted in suspending the market forces which could serve to prevent a return of the expansion, in the form of a new boom, and the crisis which inevitably follows. If the banks emerge from the crisis unscathed, or only slightly weakened, what remains to restrain them from embarking once more on an attempt to reduce artificially the interest rate on loans and expand circulation credit? If the crisis were ruthlessly permitted to run its course, bringing about the destruction of enterprises which were unable to meet their obligations, then all entrepreneurs—not only banks but also other businessmen—would exhibit more caution in granting and using credit in the future. Instead, public opinion approves of giving assistance in the crisis. Then, no sooner is the worst over than the banks are spurred on to a new expansion of circulation credit.

To the businessman, it appears most natural and understandable that the banks should satisfy his demand for credit by the creation of fiduciary media. The banks, he believes, should have the task and the duty to "stand by" business and trade. There is no dispute that the expansion of circulation credit furthers the accumulation of capital within the narrow limits of the "forced savings" it brings about and to that extent permits an increase in productivity. Still it can be argued that, given the situation, each step in this direction steers business activity, in the manner described above, on a "wrong" course. The discrepancy between what the entrepreneurs do and what the unhampered market would have prescribed becomes evident in the crisis. The fact that each crisis, with its unpleasant consequences, is followed once more by a new "boom," which must eventually expend itself as another crisis, is due only to the circumstances that the ideology which dominates all influential groups—political economists, politicians, statesmen, the press and the business world—not only sanctions, but also demands, the expansion of circulation credit.

IV

The Crisis Policy of the Currency School

1. The Inadequacy of the Currency School

Every advance toward explaining the problem of business fluctuations to date is due to the Currency School. We are also indebted to this School alone for the ideas responsible for policies aimed at eliminating business fluctuations. The fatal error of the Currency School consisted in the fact that it failed to recognize the similarity between banknotes and bank demand deposits as money substitutes and, thus, as money certificates and fiduciary media. In their eyes, only the banknote was a money substitute. In their view, therefore, the circulation of pure metallic money could only be adulterated by the introduction of a banknote not covered by money.

Consequently, they thought that the only thing that needed to be done to prevent the periodic return of crises was to set a rigid limit for the issue of banknotes not backed by metal. The issue of fiduciary media in the form of demand deposits not covered by metal was left free.[1] Since nothing stood in the way of granting circulation credit through bank deposits, the policy of expanding circulation credit could be continued even in England. When technical difficulties limited further bank loans and precipitated a crisis, it became customary to come to the assistance of the banks and their customers with special issues of notes. The practice of restricting the notes in circulation not covered by metal, by limiting the ratio of such notes to metal, systematized this procedure. Banks could expand the volume of credit with ease if they could count on the support of the bank of issue in an emergency.

---

1. Even the countries that have followed different procedures in this respect have, for all practical purposes, placed no obstacle in the way of the development of fiduciary media in the form of bank deposits.

If all further expansion of fiduciary media had been forbidden in any form, that is, if the banks had been obliged to hold full reserves for both the additional notes issued and increases in customers' demand deposits subject to check or similar claim—or at least had not been permitted to increase the quantity of fiduciary media beyond a strictly limited ratio—prices would have declined sharply, especially at times when the increased demand for money surpassed the increase in its quantity. The economy would then not only have lacked the drive contributed by any "forced savings," it would also have temporarily suffered from the consequences of a rise in the monetary unit's purchasing power [i.e., falling prices]. Capital accumulation would then have been slowed down, although certainly not stopped. In any case, the economy surely would not then have experienced periods of stormy upswings followed by dramatic reversals of the upswings into crises and declines.

There is little sense in discussing whether it would have been better to restrict, in this way, the issue of fiduciary media by the banks than it was to pursue the policy actually followed. The alternatives are not merely restriction or freedom in the issue of fiduciary media. The alternatives are, or at least were, privilege in the granting of fiduciary media or true free banking.

The possibility of free banking has scarcely even been suggested. Intervention cast its first shadow over the capitalistic system when banking policy came to the forefront of economic and political discussion. To be sure, some authors, who defended free banking, appeared on the scene. However, their voices were overpowered. The desired goal was to protect the noteholders against the banks. It was forgotten that those hurt by the dangerous suspension of payments by the banks of issue are always the very ones the law was intended to help. No matter how severe the consequences one may anticipate from a breakdown of the banks under a system of absolutely free banking, one would have to admit that they could never even remotely approach the severity of those brought about by the war and postwar banking policies of the three European empires.[2]

---

2. [An informal alliance of Austria-Hungary, Germany, and Russia, known as the "Three Emperors' League" (1872). Its influence was declining by 1890, and World War I dealt it a final blow.—Ed.]

2. "Booms" Favored

In the last two generations, hardly anyone who has given this matter some thought can fail to know that a crisis follows a boom. Nevertheless, it would have been impossible for even the sharpest and cleverest banker to suppress in time the expansion of circulation credit. Public opinion stood in the way. The fact that business conditions fluctuated violently was generally assumed to be inherent in the capitalistic system. Under the influence of the Banking Theory, it was thought that the banks merely went along with the upswing and that their conduct had nothing to do with bringing it about or advancing it. If, after a long period of stagnation, the banks again began to respond to the general demand for easier credit, public opinion was always delighted by the signs of the start of a boom.

In view of the prevailing ideology, it would have been completely unthinkable for the banks to apply the brakes at the start of such a boom. If business conditions continued to improve, then, in conformity with the principles of Lord Overstone, prophecies of a reaction certainly increased in number. However, even those who gave this warning usually did not call for a rigorous halt to all further expansion of circulation credit. They asked only for moderation and for restricting newly granted credits to "non-speculative" businesses.

Then finally, if the banks changed their policy and the crisis came, it was always easy to find culprits. But there was no desire to locate the real offender—the false theoretical doctrine. So no changes were made in traditional procedures. Economic waves continued to follow one another.

The managers of the banks of issue have carried out their policy without reflecting very much on its basis. If the expansion of circulation credit began to alarm them, they proceeded, not always very skillfully, to raise the discount rate. Thus, they exposed themselves to public censure for having initiated the crisis by their behavior. It is clear that the crisis must come sooner or later. It is also clear that the crisis must always be caused, primarily and directly, by the change in the conduct of the banks. If we speak of error on the part of the banks, however, we must point to the wrong they do in encouraging the upswing. The fault lies not with the policy of raising the interest rate, but only with the fact that it was raised too late.

V

Modern Cyclical Policy

1.   Pre–World War I Policy

The cyclical policy recommended today, in most of the literature dealing with the problem of business fluctuations and toward which considerable strides have already been made in the United States, rests entirely on the reasoning of the Circulation Credit Theory.[1] The aim of much of this literature is to make this theory useful in practice by studying business conditions with precise statistical methods.

There is no need to explain further that there is only one business cycle theory—the Circulation Credit Theory. All other attempts to cope with the problem have failed to withstand criticism. Every crisis policy and every cyclical policy has been derived from this theory. Its ideas have formed the basis of those cyclical and crisis policies pursued in the decades preceding the war. Thus, the Banking Theory, then recognized in literature as the only correct explanation, as well as all those interpretations which related the problem to the theory of direct exchange, were already disregarded. It may have still been popular to speak of the elasticity of notes in circulation as depending on the discounting of commodity bills of exchange. However, in the world of the bank managers, who made cyclical policy, other views prevailed.

To this extent, therefore, one cannot say that the theory behind today's cyclical policy is new. The Circulation Credit Theory has, to be sure, come a long way from the old Currency Theory. The studies which Walras, Wicksell and I have devoted to the problem have

---

1. [The United States Federal Reserve System, established in 1913, was intended to limit monetary expansion. It responded to the post–World War I boom by raising the discount rate, bringing an end to credit expansion and precipitating the 1920–1921 correction period, or "recession."—Ed.]

conceived of it as a more general phenomenon. These studies have related it to the whole economic process. They have sought to deal with it especially as a problem of interest rate formulation and of "equilibrium" on the loan market. To recognize the extent of the progress made, compare, for instance, the famous controversy over free credit between Bastiat and Proudhon.[2] Or compare the usual criticism of the Quantity Theory in prewar German literature with recent discussions on the subject. However, no matter how significant this progress may be considered for the development of our understanding, we should not forget that the Currency Theory had already offered policy making every assistance in this regard that a theory can.

It is certainly not to be disputed that substantial progress was made when the problem was considered, not only from the point of view of fiduciary media, but from that of the entire problem of the purchasing power of money. The Currency School paid attention to price changes only insofar as they were produced by an increase or decrease of circulation credit—but they considered only the circulation credit granted by the issue of notes. Thus, the Currency School was a long way from striving for stabilization of the purchasing power of the monetary unit.

2.   Post–World War I Policies

Today these two problems, the issuance of fiduciary media and the purchasing power of the monetary unit, are seen as being closely linked to the Circulation Credit Theory. One of the tendencies of modern cyclical policy is that these two problems are treated as one. Thus, one aim of cyclical policy is no more nor less than the stabilization of the purchasing power of money. For a discussion of this see Part I of this study.

Like the Currency School, the other aim is not to stabilize purchasing power but only to avoid the crisis. However, a still further goal is contemplated—similar to that sought by the Peel Act and by prewar cy-

2. [Frédéric Bastiat (1801–1850) replied to an open letter addressed to him by an editor of *Voix du Peuple* (October 22, 1849). Then the socialist Pierre Jean Proudhon (1809–1865), answered. Proudhon, an advocate of unlimited monetary expansion by reduction of the interest rate to zero, and Bastiat, who favored moderate credit expansion and only a limited reduction of interest rates, carried on a lengthy exchange for several months, until March 7, 1850. (*Oeuvres Complètes de Frédéric Bastiat.* 4th ed. Vol. 5. Paris, 1878, pp. 93–336.)—Ed.]

clical policy. It is proposed to counteract a boom, whether caused by an expansion of fiduciary media or by a monetary inflation (for example, an increase in the production of gold). Then again, depression is to be avoided when there is restriction irrespective of whether it starts with a contraction in the quantity of money or of fiduciary media. The aim is not to keep prices stable, but to prevent the free market interest rate from being reduced temporarily by the banks of issue or by monetary inflation.

In order to explain the essence of this new policy, we shall now explore two specific cases in more detail:

1. The production of gold increases and prices rise. A price premium appears in the interest rate that would limit the demand for loans to the supply of lendable funds available. The banks, however, have no reason to raise their lending rate. As a matter of fact, they become more willing to discount at a lower rate as the relationship between their obligations and their stock of gold has been improved. It has certainly not deteriorated. The actual loan rate they are asking lags behind the interest rate that would prevail on a free market, thus providing the initiative for a boom. In this instance, prewar crisis policy would not have intervened since it considered only the ratio of the bank's cover which had not deteriorated. As prices and wages rise [resulting in an increased demand for business loans], modern theory maintains that the interest rates should rise and circulation credit be restricted.

2. The inducement to the boom has been given by the banks in response, let us say, to the general pressure to make credit cheaper in order to combat depression, without any change in the quantity of money in the narrower sense. Since the cover ratio deteriorates as a result, even the older crisis policy would have called for increasing the interest rate as a brake.

Only in the first of these two instances does a fundamental difference exist between old and new policies.

3. Empirical Studies

Many now engaged in cyclical research maintain that the special superiority of current crisis policy in America rests on the use of more precise statistical methods than those previously available. Presumably, means for eliminating seasonal fluctuations and the secular general trend have been developed from statistical series and curves. Obviously, it is only with such manipulations that the findings of a market study may become a study of the business cycle. However, even if one should agree with the American investigators in their evaluation of the success of this effort, the question remains as to the usefulness of index numbers. Nothing more can be added to what has been said above on the subject, in Part I of this study.

The development of the Three Market Barometer[3] is considered the most important accomplishment of the Harvard investigations. Since it is not possible to determine Wicksell's natural rate of interest or the "ideal" price premium, we are advised to compare the change in the interest rate with the movement of prices and other data indicative of business conditions, such as production figures, the number of unemployed, etc. This has been done for decades. One need only glance at reports in the daily papers, economic weeklies, monthlies and annuals of the last two generations to discover that the many claims, made so proudly today, of being the first to recognize the significance of such data for understanding the course of business conditions are unwarranted. The Harvard institute, however, has performed a service in that it has sought to establish an empirical regularity in the timing of the movements in the three curves.

There is no need to share the exuberant expectations for the practical usefulness of the Harvard barometer which has prevailed in the American business world for some time. It can readily be admitted that this barometer has scarcely contributed anything toward increasing and deepening our knowledge of cyclical movements. Nevertheless, the significance of the Harvard barometer for the investigation of business conditions may still be highly valued, for it does provide statistical substantiation of the Circulation Credit Theory. Twenty years ago, it would not have been thought possible to arrange and manipulate statistical material so as to make it useful for the study of business conditions. Here real success has crowned the ingenious work done by economists and statisticians together.

Upon examining the curves developed by institutes using the Harvard method, it becomes apparent that the movement of the money market curve (C Curve) in relation to the stock market curve (A Curve)

3. [This Harvard barometer was developed at the university by the Committee on Economic Research from three statistical series which are presumed to reveal (1) the extent of stock speculation, (2) the condition of industry and trade and (3) the supply of funds.—Ed.]

and the commodity market curve (B Curve) corresponds exactly to what the Circulation Credit Theory asserts. The fact that the movements of A Curve generally anticipate those of B Curve is explained by the greater sensitivity of stock, as opposed to commodity, speculation. The stock market reacts more promptly than does the commodity market. It sees more and it sees farther. It is quicker to draw coming events (in this case, the changes in the interest rate) into the sphere of its conjectures.

4.   Arbitrary Political Decisions

However, the crucial question still remains: What does the Three Market Barometer offer the man who is actually making bank policy? Are modern methods of studying business conditions better suited than the former, to be sure less thorough, ones for laying the groundwork for decisions on a discount policy aimed at reducing as much as possible the ups and downs of business? Even prewar [World War I] banking policy had this for its goal. There is no doubt that government agencies responsible for financial policy, directors of the central banks of issue and also of the large private banks and banking houses, were frankly and sincerely interested in attaining this goal. Their efforts in this direction—only when the boom was already in full swing to be sure— were supported at least by a segment of public opinion and of the press. They knew well enough what was needed to accomplish the desired effect. They knew that nothing but a timely and sufficiently far-reaching increase in the loan rate could counteract what was usually referred to as "excessive speculation."

They failed to recognize the fundamental problem. They did not understand that every increase in the amount of circulation credit (whether brought about by the issue of banknotes or expanding bank deposits) causes a surge in business and thus starts the cycle which leads once more, over and beyond the crisis, to the decline in business activity. In short, they embraced the very ideology responsible for generating business fluctuations. However, this fact did not prevent them, once the cyclical upswing became obvious, from thinking about its unavoidable outcome. They did not know that the upswing had been generated by the conduct of the banks. If they had, they might well have seen it only as a blessing of banking policy, for to them the most important task of economic policy was to overcome the depression, at least so long as the depression lasted. Still they knew that a progressing upswing must lead to crisis and then to stagnation.

As a result, the trade boom evoked misgivings at once. The immediate problem became simply how to counteract the onward course of the "unhealthy" development. There was no question of "whether," but only of "how." Since the method—increasing the interest rate—was already settled, the question of "how" was only a matter of timing and degree: When and how much should the interest rate be raised?

The critical point was that this question could not be answered precisely, on the basis of undisputed data. As a result, the decision must always be left to discretionary judgment. Now, the more firmly convinced those responsible were that their interference, by raising the interest rate, would put an end to the prosperity of the boom, the more cautiously they must act. Might not those voices be correct which maintained that the upswing was *not* "artificially" produced, that there wasn't any "overspeculation" at all, that the boom was only the natural outgrowth of technical progress, the development of means of communication, the discovery of new supplies of raw materials, the opening up of new markets? Should this delightful and happy state of affairs be rudely interrupted? Should the government act in such a way that the economic improvement, for which it took credit, gives way to crisis?

The hesitation of officials to intervene is sufficient to explain the situation. To be sure, they had the best of intentions for stopping in time. Even so, the steps they took were usually "too little and too late." There was always a time lag before the interest rate reached the point at which prices must start down again. In the interim, capital had become frozen in investments for which it would not have been used if the interest rate on money had not been held below its "natural rate."

This drawback to cyclical policy is not changed in any respect if it is carried out in accordance with the business barometer. No one who has carefully studied the conclusions drawn from observations of business conditions made by institutions working with modern methods will dare to contend that these results may be used to establish, incontrovertibly, when and how much to raise the interest rate in order to end the boom in time before it has led to capital malinvestment. The accomplishment of economic journalism in reporting regularly on business conditions during the last two generations should not be *under*rated. Nor should the contribution of contemporary business cycle research institutes, working with substantial means, be *over*rated. Despite all the improvements which the preparation of statistics and graphic interpretations have undergone, their use in the determination of interest rate policy still leaves a wide margin for judgment.

5. Sound Theory Essential

Moreover, it should not be forgotten that it is impossible to answer in a straightforward manner not only how seasonal variations and growth factors are to be eliminated, but also how to decide unequivocally from what data and by what method the curves of each of the Three Markets should be constructed. Arguments which cannot be easily refuted may be raised on every point with respect to the business barometer. Also, no matter how much the business barometer may help us to survey the many heterogeneous operations of the market and of production, they certainly do not offer a solid basis for weighing contingencies. Business barometers are not even in a position to furnish clear and certain answers to the questions concerning cyclical policy which are crucial for their operation. Thus, the great expectations generally associated with recent cyclical policy today are not justified.

For the future of cyclical policy more profound theoretical knowledge concerning the nature of changes in business conditions would inevitably be of incomparably greater value than any conceivable manipulation of statistical methods. Some business cycle research institutes are imbued with the erroneous idea that they are conducting impartial factual research, free of any prejudice due to theoretical considerations. In fact, all their work rests on the groundwork of the Circulation Credit Theory. In spite of the reluctance which exists today against logical reasoning in economics and against thinking problems and theories through to their ultimate conclusions, a great deal would be gained if it were decided to base cyclical policy deliberately on this theory. Then, one would know that every expansion of circulation credit must be counteracted in order to even out the waves of the business cycle. Then, a force operating on one side to reduce the purchasing power of money would be offset from the other side. The difficulties, due to the impossibility of finding any method for measuring changes in purchasing power, cannot be overcome. It is impossible to realize the ideal of either a monetary unit of unchanging value or economic stability. However, once it is resolved to forego the artificial stimulation of business activity by means of banking policy, fluctuations in business conditions will surely be substantially reduced. To be sure this will mean giving up many a well-loved slogan, for example, "easy money" to encourage credit transactions. However, a still greater ideological sacrifice than that is called for. *The desire to reduce the interest rate in any way must also be abandoned.*

It has already been pointed out that events would have turned out very differently if there had been no deviation from the principle of complete freedom in banking and if the issue of fiduciary media had been in no way exempted from the rules of commercial law. It may be that a final solution of the problem can be arrived at only through the establishment of completely free banking. However, the credit structure which has been developed by the continued effort of many generations cannot be transformed with one blow. Future generations, who will have recognized the basic absurdity of all interventionist attempts, will have to deal with this question also. However, the time is not yet ripe—not now nor in the immediate future.

VI

Control of the Money Market

1.   International Competition or Cooperation

There are many indications that public opinion has recognized the significance of the role banks play in initiating the cycle by their expansion of circulation credit. If this view should actually prevail, then the previous popularity of efforts aimed at artificially reducing the interest rate on loans would disappear. Banks that wanted to expand their issue of fiduciary media would no longer be able to count on public approval or government support. They would become more careful and more temperate. That would smooth out the waves of the cycle and reduce the severity of the sudden shift from rise to fall.

However, there are some indications which seem to contradict this view of public opinion. Most important among these are the attempts or, more precisely, the reasoning which underlies the attempts to bring about international cooperation among the banks of issue.

In speculative periods of the past, the very fact that the banks of the various countries did not work together systematically and according to agreement constituted a most effective brake. With closely-knit international economic relations, the expansion of circulation credit could only become universal if it were an international phenomenon. Accordingly, lacking any international agreement, individual banks, fearing a large outflow of capital, took care in setting their interest rates not to lag far below the rates of the banks of other countries. Thus, in response to interest rate arbitrage and any deterioration in the balance of trade brought about by higher prices, an exodus of loan money to other countries would, for one thing, have impaired the ratio of the bank's cover as a result of foreign claims on their gold and foreign exchange which such conditions impose on the bank of issue. The bank, obliged to consider its solvency, would then be forced to restrict credit.

In addition, this impairment of the ever-shifting balance of payments would create a shortage of funds on the money market which the banks would be powerless to combat. The closer the economic connections among peoples become, the less possible it is to have a *national* boom. The business climate becomes an *international* phenomenon.

However, in many countries, especially in the German Reich, the view has frequently been expressed by friends of "cheap money" that it is only the gold standard that forces the bank of issue to consider interest rates abroad in determining its own interest policy. According to this view, if the bank were free of this shackle, it could then better satisfy the demands of the domestic money market to the advantage of the national economy. With this view in mind, there were in Germany advocates of bimetallism, as well as of a gold premium policy.[1] In Austria, there was resistance to formalizing legally the *de facto* practice of redeeming its notes.

It is easy to see the fallacy in this doctrine that only the tie of the monetary unit to gold keeps the banks from reducing interest rates at will. Even if all ties with the gold standard were broken, this would not have given the banks the power to lower with impunity the interest rate below the height of the "natural" interest rate. To be sure, the paper standard would have permitted them to continue the expansion of circulation credit without hesitation, because a bank of issue, relieved of the obligation of redeeming its notes, need have no fear with respect to its solvency. Still, the increase in notes would have led first to price increases and consequently to a deterioration in the rate of exchange. Secondly, the crisis would have come—later, to be sure, but all the more severely.

If the banks of issue were to consider seriously making agreements with respect to discount policy, this would eliminate one effective check. By acting in unison, the banks could extend more circulation credit than they do now, without any fear that the consequences would lead to a situation which produces an external drain of funds from the money market. To be sure, if this concern with the situation abroad is eliminated, the banks are still not always in a position to reduce the money rate of interest below its "natural" rate in the long run. However, the difference between the two interest rates can be maintained longer, so that the inevitable result—malinvestment of capital—appears

1. [See above p. 40, n. 3.—Ed.]

on a larger scale. This must then intensify the unavoidable crisis and deepen the depression.

So far, it is true, the banks of issue have made no significant agreements on cyclical policy. Nevertheless, efforts aimed at such agreements are certainly being proposed on every side.

2. "Boom" Promotion Problems

Another dangerous sign is that the slogan concerning the need to "control the money market," through the banks of issue, still retains its prestige.

Given the situation, especially as it has developed in Europe, only the central banks are entitled to issue notes. Under that system, attempts to expand circulation credit universally can only originate with the central bank of issue. Every venture on the part of private banks, against the wish or the plan of the central bank, is doomed from the very beginning. Even banking techniques learned from the Anglo-Saxons are of no service to private banks, since the opportunity for granting credit by opening bank deposits is insignificant in countries where the use of checks (except for central bank clearings and the circulation of postal checks) is confined to a narrow circle in the business world. However, if the central bank of issue embarks upon a policy of credit expansion and thus begins to force down the rate of interest, it may be advantageous for the largest private banks to follow suit and expand the volume of circulation credit *they* grant too. Such a procedure has still a further advantage for them. It involves them in no risk. If confidence is shaken during the crisis, they can survive the critical stage with the aid of the bank of issue.

However, the bank of issue's credit expansion policy certainly offers a large number of banks a profitable field for speculation—arbitrage in the loan rates of interest. They seek to profit from the shifting ratio between domestic and foreign interest rates by investing domestically obtained funds in short-term funds abroad. In this process, they are acting in opposition to the discount policy of the bank of issue and hurting the alleged interests of those groups which hope to benefit from the artificial reduction of the interest rate and from the boom it produces. The ideology, which sees salvation in every effort to lower the interest rate and regards expansion of circulation credit as the best method of attaining this goal, is consistent with the policy of branding the actions of the interest rate arbitrageur as scandalous and disgraceful, even as a betrayal of the interests of his own people to the advantage of foreigners. The policy of granting the banks of issue every possible assistance in the fight against these speculators is also consistent with this ideology. Both government and bank of issue seek to intimidate the malefactors with threats, to dissuade them from their plan. In the liberal countries of western Europe, at least in the past, little could be accomplished by such methods. In the interventionist countries of middle and eastern Europe, attempts of this kind have met with greater success.

It is easy to see what lies behind this effort of the bank of issue to "control" the money market. The bank wants to prevent its credit expansion policy, aimed at reducing the interest rate, from being impeded by consideration of relatively restrictive policies followed abroad. It seeks to promote a domestic boom without interference from international reactions.

3.   Drive for Tighter Controls

According to the prevailing ideology, however, there are still other occasions when the banks of issue should have stronger control over the money market. If the interest rate arbitrage, resulting from the expansion of circulation credit, has led, for the time being, only to a withdrawal of funds from the reserves of the issuing bank, and that bank, disconcerted by the deterioration of the security behind its notes, has proceeded to raise its discount rate, there may still be, under certain conditions, no cause for the loan rate to rise on the open money market. As yet no funds have been withdrawn from the domestic market. The gold exports came from the bank's reserves, and the increase in the discount rate has not led to a reduction in the credits granted by the bank. It takes time for loan funds to become scarce as a result of the fact that some commercial paper, which would otherwise have been offered to the bank for discount, is disposed of on the open market. The issuing bank, however, does not want to wait so long for its maneuver to be effective. Alarmed at the state of its gold and foreign exchange assets, it wants prompt relief. To accomplish this, it must try to make money scarce on the market. It generally tries to bring this about by appearing itself as a borrower on the market.

Another case, when control of the money market is contested, concerns the utilization of funds made available to the market by the generous discount policy. The dominant ideology favors "cheap money." It also favors high commodity prices, but not always high stock market prices. The moderated interest rate is intended to stimulate production and not to cause a stock market boom. However, stock prices increase first of all. At the outset, commodity prices are not caught up in the boom. There are stock exchange booms and stock exchange profits. Yet, the "producer" is dissatisfied. He envies the "speculator" his "easy profit." Those in power are not willing to accept this situation. They believe that production is being deprived of money which is flowing into the stock market. Besides, it is precisely in the stock market boom that the serious threat of a crisis lies hidden.

Therefore, the aim is to withdraw money from stock exchange loans in order to inject it into the "economy." Trying to do this simply by raising the interest rate offers no special attraction. Such a rise in the interest rate is certainly unavoidable in the end. It is only a question of whether it comes sooner or later. Whenever the interest rate rises sufficiently, it brings an end to the business boom. Therefore, other measures are tried to transfer funds from the stock market into production without changing the cheap rate for loans. The bank of issue exerts pressure on borrowers to influence the use made of the sums loaned out. Or else it proceeds directly to set different terms for credit depending on its use.

Thus we can see what it means if the central bank of issue aims at domination of the money market. Either the expansion of circulation credit is freed from the limitations which would eventually restrict it. Or the boom is shifted by certain measures along a course different from the one it would otherwise have followed. Thus, the pressure for "control of the money market" specifically envisions the encouragement of the boom—the boom which must end in a crisis. If a cyclical policy is to be followed to eliminate crises, this desire, the desire to control and dominate the money market, must be abandoned.

If it were seriously desired to counteract price increases resulting from an increase in the quantity of money—due to an increase in the mining of gold, for example—by restricting circulation credit, the central banks of issue would borrow more on the market. Paying off these obligations later could hardly be described as "controlling the money market." For the bank of issue, the restriction of circulation credit means the renunciation of profits. It may even mean losses.

Moreover, such a policy can be successful only if there is agreement among the banks of issue. If restriction were practiced by the central bank of one country only, it would result in relatively high costs of borrowing money within that country. The chief consequence of this would then be that gold would flow in from abroad. Insofar as this is the goal sought by the cooperation of the banks, it certainly cannot be considered a dangerous step in the attempt toward a policy of evening out the waves of the business cycle.

VII

Business Forecasting for Cyclical Policy and the Businessman

1.   Contributions of Business Cycle Research

The popularity enjoyed by contemporary business cycle research, the development of which is due above all to American economic researchers, derives from exaggerated expectations as to its usefulness in practice. With its help, it had been hoped to mechanize banking policy and business activity. It had been hoped that a glance at the business barometer would tell businessmen and those who determine banking policy how to act.

At present, this is certainly out of the question. It has already been emphasized often enough that the results of business cycle studies have only described past events and that they may be used for predicting future developments only on the basis of extremely inadequate principles. However—and this is not sufficiently noted—these principles apply solely on the assumption that the ideology calling for expansion of circulation credit has not lost its standing in the field of economic and banking policy. Once a serious start is made at directing cyclical policy toward the *elimination* of crises, the power of this ideology is already dissipated.

Nevertheless, one broad field remains for the employment of the results of contemporary business cycle studies. They should indicate to the makers of banking policy when the interest rate must be raised to avoid instigating credit expansion. If the study of business conditions were clear on this point and gave answers admitting of only one interpretation, so that there could be only one opinion, not only as to *whether* but also as to *when* and *how much* to increase the discount rate, then the advantage of such studies could not be rated highly enough. However, this is not the case. Everything that the observation of business conditions contributes in the form of manipulated data and material can be interpreted in various ways.

Even before the development of business barometers, it was already known that increases in stock market quotations and commodity prices, a rise in profits on raw materials, a drop in unemployment, an increase in business orders, the selling off of inventories, and so on, signified a boom. The question is, when should, or when must, the brakes be applied. However, no business cycle institute answers this question straightforwardly and without equivocation. What should be done will always depend on an examination of the driving forces which shape business conditions and on the objectives set for cyclical policy. Whether the right moment for action is seized can never be decided except on the basis of a careful observation of all market phenomena. Moreover, it has never been possible to answer this question in any other way. The fact that we now know how to classify and describe the various market data more clearly than before does not make the task essentially any easier.

A glance at the continuous reports on the economy and the stock market in the large daily newspapers and in the economic weeklies which appeared from 1840 to 1910 shows that attempts have been made for decades to draw conclusions from events of the most recent past, on the basis of empirical rules, as to the shape of the immediate future. If we compare the statistical groundwork used in these attempts with those now at our disposal, then it is obvious that we have recourse to more data today. We also understand better how to organize this material, how to arrange it clearly and interpret it for graphic presentation. However, we can by no means claim, with the modern methods of studying business conditions, to have embarked on some new principle.

2.   Difficulties of Precise Prediction

No businessman may safely neglect any available source of information. Thus no businessman can refuse to pay close attention to newspaper reports. Still diligent newspaper reading is no guarantee of business success. If success were that easy, what wealth would the journalists have already amassed! In the business world, success depends on comprehending the situation sooner than others do—and acting accordingly. What is recognized as "fact" must first be evaluated correctly to make it useful for an undertaking. Precisely this is the problem of putting theory into practice.

A prediction, which makes judgments which are *qualitative* only and not *quantitative*, is practically useless even if it is eventually proved right by the later course of events. There is also the crucial question of timing. Decades ago, Herbert Spencer recognized, with brilliant perception, that militarism, imperialism, socialism and interventionism must lead to great wars, severe wars. However, anyone who had started about 1890 to speculate on the strength of that insight on a depreciation of the bonds of the Three Empires[1] would have sustained heavy losses. Large historical perspectives furnish no basis for stock market speculations which must be reviewed daily, weekly, or monthly at least.

It is well known that every boom must one day come to an end. The businessman's situation, however, depends on knowing exactly when and where the break will first appear. No economic barometer can answer these questions. An economic barometer only furnishes data from which conclusions may be drawn. Since it is still possible for the central bank of issue to delay the start of the catastrophe with its discount policy, the situation depends chiefly on making judgments as to the conduct of these authorities. Obviously, all available data fail at this point.

But once public opinion is completely dominated by the view that the crisis is imminent and businessmen act on this basis, then it is already too late to derive business profit from this knowledge. Or even merely to avoid losses. For then the panic breaks out. The crisis has come.

---

1. [See above, p. 129, n. 2.—Ed.]

VIII

The Aims and Method of Cyclical Policy

1.   Revised Currency School Theory

Without doubt, expanding the sphere of scientific investigation from the narrow problem of the crisis into the broader problem of the cycle represents progress.[1] However, it was certainly not equally advantageous for political policies. Their scope was broadened. They began to aspire to more than was feasible.

The economy could be organized so as to eliminate cyclical changes only if (1) there were something more than muddled thinking behind the concept that changes in the value of the monetary unit can be measured, and (2) it were possible to determine in advance the extent of the effect which accompanies a definite change in the quantity of money and fiduciary media. As these conditions do not prevail, the goals of cyclical policy must be more limited. However, even if only such severe shocks as those experienced in 1857, 1873, 1900/01 and 1907 could be avoided in the future, a great deal would have been accomplished.

The most important prerequisite of any cyclical policy, no matter how modest its goal may be, is to renounce every attempt to reduce the interest rate, by means of banking policy, below the rate which develops on the market. That means a return to the theory of the Currency School, which sought to suppress all future expansion of circulation credit and thus all further creation of fiduciary media. However, this does not mean a return to the old Currency School program, the application of which was limited to banknotes. Rather it means the introduction of a new program based on the old Currency School theory,

---

1. Also, as a result of this, it became easier to distinguish crises originating from definite causes (wars and political upheavals, violent convulsions of nature, changes in the shape of supply or demand) from cyclically-recurring crises.

but expanded in the light of the present state of knowledge to include fiduciary media issued in the form of bank deposits.

The banks would be obliged at all times to maintain metallic backing for all notes—except for the sum of those outstanding which are not now covered by metal—equal to the total sum of the notes issued and bank deposits opened. That would mean a complete reorganization of central bank legislation. The banks of issue would have to return to the principles of Peel's Bank Act, but with the provisions expanded to cover also bank balances subject to check. The same stipulations with respect to reserves must also be applied to the large national deposit institutions, especially the postal savings.[2] Of course, for these secondary banks of issue, the central bank reserves for their notes and deposits would be the equivalent of gold reserves. In those countries where checking accounts at private commercial banks play an important role in trade—notably the United States and England—the same obligation must be exacted from those banks also.

By this act alone, cyclical policy would be directed in earnest toward the elimination of crises.

2.   "Price Level" Stabilization

Under present circumstances, it is out of the question, in the foreseeable future, to establish complete "free banking" and place all banking transactions, including the granting of credit, under ordinary commercial law. Those who speak and write today on behalf of "stabilization," "maintenance of purchasing power" and "elimination of the trade cycle" can certainly not call this more limited approach "extreme." On the contrary! They will reject this suggestion as not going far enough. They are demanding much more. In their view, the "price level" should be maintained by countering rising prices with a restriction in the circulation of fiduciary media and, similarly, countering falling prices by the expansion of fiduciary media.

The arguments that may be advanced *in favor of* this modest program have already been set forth above in the first part of this work. In our judgment, the arguments which militate *against* all monetary

2. [The Post Office Savings Institution, established in Austria in the 1880s and copied in several other European countries, played a significant, if limited, role in monetary affairs. See Mises's comments in *Human Action* (1966, 1996, and 2007), pp. 445–446.—Ed.]

manipulation are so great that placing decisions as to the formation of purchasing power in the hands of banking officials, parliaments and governments, thus making it subject to shifting political influences, must be avoided. The methods available for measuring changes in purchasing power are necessarily defective. The effect of the various maneuvers, intended to influence purchasing power, cannot be quantitatively established—neither in advance nor even after they have taken place. Thus proposals which amount only to making approximate adjustments in purchasing power must be considered completely impractical.

Nothing more will be said here concerning the fundamental absurdity of the concept of "stable purchasing power" in a changing economy. This has already been discussed at some length. For practical economic policy, the only problem is what inflationist or restrictionist measures to consider for the partial adjustment of severe price declines or increases. Such measures, carried out in stages, step by step, through piecemeal international agreements, would benefit either creditors or debtors. However, one question remains: Whether, in view of the conflicts among interests, agreements on this issue could be reached among nations. The viewpoints of creditors and debtors will no doubt differ widely, and these conflicts of interest will complicate still more the manipulation of money internationally than on the national level.

3.   International Complications

It is also possible to consider monetary manipulation as an aspect of national economic policy, and take steps to regulate the value of money independently, without reference to the international situation. According to Keynes,[3] if there is a choice between stabilization of prices and stabilization of the foreign exchange rate, the decision should be in favor of price stabilization and against stabilization of the rate of exchange. However, a nation which chose to proceed in this way would create international complications because of the repercussions its policy would have on the content of contractual obligations.

For example, if the United States were to raise the purchasing power

---

3. Keynes, John Maynard. *A Tract on Monetary Reform.* London, 1923; New York, 1924, pp. 156ff.

of the dollar over that of its present gold parity, the interests of foreigners who owed dollars would be very definitely affected as a result. Then again, if debtor nations were to try to depress the purchasing power of their monetary unit, the interests of creditors would be impaired. Irrespective of this, every change in value of a monetary unit would unleash influences on foreign trade. A rise in its value would foster increased imports, while a fall in its value would be recognized as the power to increase exports.

In recent generations, consideration of these factors has led to pressure for a single monetary standard based on gold. If this situation is ignored, then it will certainly not be possible to fashion monetary value so that it will generally be considered satisfactory. In view of the ideas prevailing today with respect to trade policy, especially in connection with foreign relations, a rising value for money is not considered desirable, because of its power to promote imports and to hamper exports.

Attempts to introduce a national policy, so as to influence prices independently of what is happening abroad, while still clinging to the gold standard and the corresponding rates of exchange, would be completely unworkable. There is no need to say any more about this.

4.   The Future

The obstacles which militate against a policy aimed at the complete elimination of cyclical changes are truly considerable. For that reason, it is not very likely that such new approaches to monetary and banking policy, that limit the creation of fiduciary media, will be followed. It will probably not be resolved to prohibit entirely the expansion of fiduciary media. Nor is it likely that expansion will be limited to only the quantities sufficient to counteract a definite and pronounced trend toward generally declining prices. Perplexed as to how to evaluate the serious political and economic doubts which are raised in opposition to every kind of manipulation of the value of money, the people will probably forego decisive action and leave it to the central bank managers to proceed, case by case, at their own discretion. Just as in the past, cyclical policy of the near future will be surrendered into the hands of the men who control the conduct of the great central banks and those who influence their ideas, i.e., the moulders of public opinion.

Nevertheless, the cyclical policy of the future will differ appreciably from its predecessor. It will be knowingly based on the Circulation Credit Theory of the Trade Cycle. The hopeless attempt to reduce the loan rate indefinitely by continuously expanding circulation credit will not be revived in the future. It may be that the quantity of fiduciary media will be intentionally expanded or contracted in order to influence purchasing power. However, the people will no longer be under the illusion that technical banking procedures can make credit cheaper and thus create prosperity without its having repercussions.

The only way to do away with, or even to alleviate, the periodic return of the trade cycle—with its denouement, the crisis—is to reject the fallacy that prosperity can be produced by using banking procedures to make credit cheap.

❧ The Causes of the Economic Crisis

An Address

The Nature and Role of the Market

1.   The Marxian "Anarchy of Production" Myth

The Marxian critique censures the capitalistic social order for the anarchy and planlessness of its production methods. Allegedly, every entrepreneur produces blindly, guided only by his desire for profit, without any concern as to whether his action satisfies a need. Thus, for Marxists, it is not surprising if severe disturbances appear again and again in the form of periodical economic crises. They maintain it would be futile to fight against all this with capitalism. It is their contention that only socialism will provide the remedy by replacing the anarchistic profit economy with a planned economic system aimed at the satisfaction of needs.

Strictly speaking, the reproach that the market economy is "anarchistic" says no more than that it is just not socialistic. That is, the actual management of production is not surrendered to a central office which directs the employment of all factors of production, but this is left to entrepreneurs and owners of the means of production. Calling the capitalistic economy "anarchistic," therefore, means only that capitalistic production is not a function of governmental institutions.

Yet, the expression "anarchy" carries with it other connotations. We usually use the word "anarchy" to refer to social conditions in which, for lack of a governmental apparatus of force to protect peace and respect for the law, the chaos of continual conflict prevails. The word "anarchy," therefore, is associated with the concept of intolerable conditions. Marxian theorists delight in using such expressions. Marxian theory needs the implications such expressions give to arouse the emo-

[*Die Ursachen der Wirtschaftskrise: Ein Vortrag* (Tübingen: J. C. B. Mohr, Paul Siebeck, 1931). Presented February 28, 1931, at Teplitz-Schönau, Czechoslovakia, before an assembly of German industrialists (Deutscher Hauptverband der Industrie).—Ed.]

tional sympathies and antipathies that are likely to hinder critical analysis. The "anarchy of production" slogan has performed this service to perfection. Whole generations have permitted it to confuse them. It has influenced the economic and political ideas of all currently active political parties and, to a remarkable extent, even those parties which loudly proclaim themselves anti-Marxist.

2.   The Role and Rule of Consumers

Even if the capitalistic method of production were "anarchistic," i.e., lacking systematic regulation from a central office, and even if individual entrepreneurs and capitalists did, in the hope of profit, direct their actions independently of one another, it is still completely wrong to suppose they have no guide for arranging production to satisfy need. It is inherent in the nature of the capitalistic economy that, in the final analysis, the employment of the factors of production is aimed only toward serving the wishes of consumers. In allocating labor and capital goods, the entrepreneurs and the capitalists are bound, by forces they are unable to escape, to satisfy the needs of consumers as fully as possible, given the state of economic wealth and technology. Thus, the contrast drawn between the capitalistic method of production, as production for profit, and the socialistic method, as production for use, is completely misleading. In the capitalistic economy, it is consumer demand that determines the pattern and direction of production, precisely because entrepreneurs and capitalists *must* consider the profitability of their enterprises.

An economy based on private ownership of the factors of production becomes meaningful through the market. The market operates by shifting the height of prices so that again and again demand and supply will tend to coincide. If demand for a good goes up, then its price rises, and this price rise leads to an increase in supply. Entepreneurs try to produce those goods the sale of which offers them the highest possible gain. They expand production of any particular item up to the point at which it ceases to be profitable. If the entrepreneur produces only those goods whose sale gives promise of yielding a profit, this means that they are producing no commodities for the manufacture of which labor and capital goods must be used which are needed for the manufacture of other commodities more urgently desired by consumers.

In the final analysis, it is the consumers who decide what shall be produced, and how. The law of the market compels entrepreneurs and capitalists to obey the orders of consumers and to fulfill their wishes with the least expenditure of time, labor and capital goods. Competition on the market sees to it that entrepreneurs and capitalists, who are not up to this task, will lose their position of control over the production process. If they cannot survive in competition, that is, in satisfying the wishes of consumers cheaper and better, then they suffer losses which diminish their importance in the economic process. If they do not soon correct the shortcomings in the management of their enterprise and capital investment, they are eliminated completely through the loss of their capital and entrepreneurial position. Henceforth, they must be content as employees with a more modest role and reduced income.

3.   Production for Consumption

The law of the market applies to labor also. Like other factors of production, labor is also valued according to its usefulness in satisfying human wants. Its price, the wage rate, is a market phenomenon like any other market phenomenon, determined by supply and demand, by the value the product of labor has in the eye of consumers. By shifting the height of wages, the market directs workers into those branches of production in which they are most urgently needed. Thus the market supplies to each type of employment that quality and quantity of labor needed to satisfy consumer wants in the best possible way.

In the feudal society, men became rich by war and conquest and through the largesse of the sovereign ruler. Men became poor if they were defeated in battle or if they fell from the monarch's good graces. In the capitalistic society, men become rich—directly as the producer of consumers' goods, or indirectly as the producer of raw materials and semi-produced factors of production—by serving consumers in large numbers. This means that men who become rich in the capitalistic society are serving the people. The capitalistic market economy is a democracy in which every penny constitutes a vote. The wealth of the successful businessman is the result of a consumer plebiscite. Wealth, once acquired, can be preserved only by those who keep on earning it anew by satisfying the wishes of consumers.

The capitalistic social order, therefore, is an economic democracy in the strictest sense of the word. In the last analysis, all decisions are dependent on the will of the people as consumers. Thus, whenever there is a conflict between consumers' views and those of the business managers, market pressures assure that the views of the consumers win out eventually. This is certainly something very different from the pseudo-economic democracy toward which the labor unions are aiming. In such a system as they propose, the people are supposed to direct production as producers, not as consumers. They would exercise influence, not as buyers of products, but as sellers of labor, that is, as sellers of one of the factors of production. If this system were carried out, it would disorganize the entire production apparatus and thus destroy our civilization. The absurdity of this position becomes apparent simply upon considering that production is not an end in itself. Its purpose is to serve consumption.

4.   The Perniciousness of a "Producers' Policy"

Under pressure of the market, entrepreneurs and capitalists must order production so as to carry out the wishes of consumers. The arrangements they make and what they ask of workers are always determined by the need to satisfy the most urgent wants of consumers. It is precisely this which guarantees that the will of the consumer shall be the only guideline for business. Yet capitalism is usually reproached for placing the logic of expediency above sentiment and arranging things in the economy dispassionately and impersonally for monetary profit only. It is because the market compels the entrepreneur to conduct his business so that he derives from it the greatest possible return that the wants of consumers are covered in the best and cheapest way. If potential profit were no longer taken into consideration by enterprises, but instead the workers' wishes became the criterion, so that work was arranged for *their* greatest convenience, then the interests of consumers would be injured. If the entrepreneur aims at the highest possible profit, he performs a service to society in managing an enterprise. Whoever hinders him from doing this, in order to give preference to considerations other than those of business profits, acts against the interests of society and imperils the satisfaction of consumer needs.

Workers and consumers are, of course, identical. If we distinguish between them, we are only differentiating mentally between their respective functions within the economic framework. We should not let this lead us into the error of thinking they are different groups of people. The fact that entrepreneurs and capitalists also are consuming plays a less important role quantitatively; for the market economy, the significant consumption is mass consumption. Directly or indirectly, capitalistic production serves primarily the consumption of the masses. The only way to improve the situation of the consumer, therefore, is to make enterprises still more productive, or as people may say today, to "rationalize"[1] still further. Only if one wants to reduce consumption should one urge what is known as "producers' policy"—specifically the adoption of those measures which place the interests of producers over those of consumers.

Opposition to the economic laws which the market decrees for production must always be at the expense of consumption. This should be kept in mind whenever interventions are advocated to free producers from the necessity of complying with the market.

The market processes give meaning to the capitalistic economy. They place entrepreneurs and capitalists in the service of satisfying the wants of consumers. If the workings of these complex processes are interfered with, then disturbances are brought about which hamper the adjustment of supply to demand and lead production astray, along paths which keep them from attaining the goal of economic action— i.e., the satisfaction of wants.

These disturbances constitute the economic crisis.

1. [A loose term for a more efficient organization of industrial production through the use of more modern technical automation and mechanization. It came in time to imply that central planning and government regulation are helpful in eliminating "wasteful" competition. The term was later applied to the Nazi and Soviet plans for industrial organization.—Ed.]

II

Cyclical Changes in Business Conditions

1.   Role of Interest Rates

In our economic system, times of good business commonly alternate more or less regularly with times of bad business. Decline follows economic upswing, upswing follows decline, and so on. The attention of economic theory has quite understandably been greatly stimulated by this problem of cyclical changes in business conditions. In the beginning, several hypotheses were set forth, which could not stand up under critical examination. However, a theory of cyclical fluctuations was finally developed which fulfilled the demands legitimately expected from a scientific solution to the problem. This is the Circulation Credit Theory, usually called the Monetary Theory of the Trade Cycle. This theory is generally recognized by science. All cyclical policy measures which are taken seriously proceed from the reasoning which lies at the root of this theory.

According to the Circulation Credit Theory (Monetary Theory of the Trade Cycle), cyclical changes in business conditions stem from attempts to reduce artificially the interest rates on loans through measures of banking policy—expansion of bank credit by the issue or creation of additional fiduciary media (that is banknotes and/or checking deposits not covered 100% by gold). On a market which is not disturbed by the interference of such an "inflationist" banking policy, interest rates develop at which the means are available to carry out all the plans and enterprises that are initiated. Such unhampered market interest rates are known as "natural" or "static" interest rates. If these interest rates were adhered to, then economic development would proceed without interruption—except for the influence of natural cataclysms of political acts such as war, revolution, and the like. The fact that economic development follows a wavy pattern must be attributed to the intervention of the banks through their interest rate policy.

The point of view prevails generally among politicians, business people, the press and public opinion that reducing the interest rates below those developed by market conditions is a worthy goal for economic policy, and that the simplest way to reach this goal is through expanding bank credit. Under the influence of this view, the attempt is undertaken, again and again, to spark an economic upswing through granting additional loans. At first, to be sure, the result of such credit expansion comes up to expectations. Business is revived. An upswing develops. However, the stimulating effect emanating from the credit expansion cannot continue forever. Sooner or later, a business boom created in this way must collapse.

At the interest rates which developed on the market, before any interference by the banks through the creation of additional circulation credit, only those enterprises and businesses appeared profitable for which the needed factors of production were available in the economy. The interest rates are reduced through the expansion of credit, and then some businesses, which did not previously seem profitable, appear to be profitable. It is precisely the fact that such businesses are undertaken that initiates the upswing. However, the economy is not wealthy enough for them. The resources they need for completion are not available. The resources they need must first be withdrawn from *other* enterprises. If the means *had* been available, then the credit expansion would not have been necessary to make the new projects appear possible.

2.   The Sequel of Credit Expansion

Credit expansion cannot increase the supply of real goods. It merely brings about a rearrangement. It diverts capital investment away from the course prescribed by the state of economic wealth and market conditions. It causes production to pursue paths which it would not follow unless the economy were to acquire an increase in material goods. As a result, the upswing lacks a solid base. It is not *real* prosperity. It is *illusory* prosperity. It did not develop from an increase in economic wealth. Rather, it arose because the credit expansion created the illusion of such an increase. Sooner or later it must become apparent that this economic situation is built on sand.

Sooner or later, credit expansion, through the creation of additional fiduciary media, must come to a standstill. Even if the banks wanted to, they could not carry on this policy indefinitely, not even if they were being forced to do so by the strongest pressure from outside. The continuing increase in the quantity of fiduciary media leads to continual price increases. Inflation can continue only so long as the opinion persists that it will stop in the foreseeable future. However, once the conviction gains a foothold that the inflation will not come to a halt, then a panic breaks out. In evaluating money and commodities, the public takes anticipated price increases into account in advance. As a consequence, prices race erratically upward out of all bounds. People turn away from using money which is compromised by the increase in fiduciary media. They "flee" to foreign money, metal bars, "real values," barter. In short, the currency breaks down.

The policy of expanding credit is usually abandoned well before this critical point is reached. It is discontinued because of the situation which develops in international trade relations and also, especially, because of experiences in previous crises, which have frequently led to legal limitations on the right of the central banks to issue notes and create credit. In any event, the policy of expanding credit must come to an end—if not sooner due to a turnabout by the banks, then later in a catastrophic breakdown. The sooner the credit expansion policy is brought to a stop, the less harm will have been done by the misdirection of entrepreneurial activity, the milder the crisis and the shorter the following period of economic stagnation and general depression.

The appearance of periodically recurring economic crises is the necessary consequence of repeatedly renewed attempts to reduce the "natural" rates of interest on the market by means of banking policy. The crises will never disappear so long as men have not learned to avoid such pump-priming, because an artificially stimulated boom must inevitably lead to crisis and depression.

III

The Present Crisis

The crisis from which we are now suffering is also the outcome of a credit expansion. The present crisis is the unavoidable sequel to a boom. Such a crisis necessarily follows every boom generated by the attempt to reduce the "natural rate of interest" through increasing the fiduciary media. However, the present crisis differs in some essential points from earlier crises, just as the preceding boom differed from earlier economic upswings.

The most recent boom period did not run its course completely, at least not in Europe. Some countries and some branches of production were not generally or very seriously affected by the upswing which, in many lands, was quite turbulent. A bit of the previous depression continued, even into the upswing. On that account—in line with our theory and on the basis of past experience—one would assume that this time the crisis will be milder. However, it is certainly much more severe than earlier crises and it does not appear likely that business conditions will soon improve.

The unprofitability of many branches of production and the unemployment of a sizeable portion of the workers can obviously not be due to the slowdown in business alone. Both the unprofitability and the unemployment are being intensified right now by the general depression. However, in this postwar period, they have become lasting phenomena which do not disappear entirely even in the upswing. We are confronted here with a new problem, one that cannot be answered by the theory of cyclical changes alone.

Let us consider, first of all, unemployment.

A. UNEMPLOYMENT

1.　　The Market Wage Rate Process

Wage rates are market phenomena, just as interest rates and commodity prices are. Wage rates are determined by the productivity of labor. At the wage rates toward which the market is tending, all those seeking work find employment and all entrepreneurs find the workers they are seeking. However, the interrelated phenomena of the market from which the "static" or "natural" wage rates evolve are always undergoing changes that generate shifts in wage rates among the various occupational groups. There is also always a definite time lag before those seeking work and those offering work have found one another. As a result, there are always sure to be a certain number of unemployed.

Just as there are always houses standing empty and persons looking for housing on the unhampered market, just as there are always unsold wares in markets and persons eager to purchase wares they have not yet found, so there are always persons who are looking for work. However, on the unhampered market, this unemployment cannot attain vast proportions. Those capable of work will not be looking for work over a considerable period—many months or even years—without finding it.

If a worker goes a long time without finding the employment he seeks in his former occupation, he must either reduce the wage rate he asks or turn to some other field where he hopes to obtain a higher wage than he can now get in his former occupation. For the entrepreneur, the employment of workers is a part of doing business. If the wage rate drops, the profitability of his enterprise rises and he can employ more workers. So by reducing the wage rates they seek, workers are in a position to raise the demand for labor.

This in no way means that the market would tend to push wage rates down indefinitely. Just as competition among workers has the tendency to lower wages, so does competition among employers tend to drive them up again. Market wage rates thus develop from the interplay of demand and supply.

The force with which competition among employers affects workers may be seen very clearly by referring to the two mass migrations which characterized the nineteenth and early twentyth centuries. The oft-cited exodus from the land rested on the fact that agriculture had to release workers to industry. Agriculture could not pay the higher wage rates which industry could and which, in fact, industry *had* to offer in order to attract workers from housework, hand labor and agriculture. The migration of workers was continually out of regions where wages were held down by the inferiority of general conditions of production and into areas where the productivity made it possible to pay higher wages.

Out of every increase in productivity, the wage earner receives his share. For profitable enterprises seeking to expand, the only means available to attract more workers is to raise wage rates. The prodigious increase in the living standard of the masses that accompanied the development of capitalism is the result of the rise in real wages which kept abreast of the increase in industrial productivity.

This self-adjusting process of the market is severely disturbed now by the interference of unions whose effectiveness evolved under the protection and with the assistance of governmental power.

2.   The Labor Union Wage Rate Concept

According to labor union doctrine, wages are determined by the balance of power. According to this view, if the unions succeed in intimidating the entrepreneurs, through force or threat of force, and holding non-union workers off with the use of brute force, then wage rates can be set at whatever height desired without the appearance of any undesirable side effects. Thus, the conflict between employers and workers seems to be a struggle in which justice and morality are entirely on the side of the workers. Interest on capital and entrepreneurial profit appear to be ill-gotten gains. They are alleged to come from the exploitation of the worker and should be set aside for unemployment relief. This task, according to union doctrine, should be accomplished not only by increased wage rates but also through taxes and welfare spending which, in a regime dominated by pro-labor union parties, is to be used indirectly for the benefit of the workers.

The labor unions use force to attain their goals. Only union members, who ask the established union wage rate and who work according to union-prescribed methods, are permitted to work in industrial undertakings. Should an employer refuse to accept union conditions, there are work stoppages. Workers who would like to work, in spite of the reproach heaped on such an undertaking by the union, are forced by acts of violence to give up any such plan. This tactic on the part of the labor unions presupposes, of course, that the government at least acquiesces in their behavior.

3.   The Cause of Unemployment

If the government were to proceed against those who molest persons willing to work and those who destroy machines and industrial equipment in enterprises that want to hire strikebreakers, as it normally does against the other perpetrators of violence, the situation would be very different. However, the characteristic feature of modern governments is that they have capitulated to the labor unions.

The unions now [1931] have the power to raise wage rates above what they would be on the unhampered market. However, interventions of this type evoke a reaction. At market wage rates, everyone looking for work can find work. Precisely this is the essence of market wages—they are established at the point at which demand and supply tend to coincide. If the wage rates are higher than this, the number of employed workers goes down. Unemployment then develops as a lasting phenomenon. At the wage rates established by the unions, a substantial portion of the workers cannot find any work at all. Wage increases for a portion of the workers are at the expense of an ever more sharply rising number of unemployed.

Those without work would probably tolerate this situation for a limited time only. Eventually they would say: "Better a lower wage than no wage at all." Even the labor unions could not withstand an assault by hundreds of thousands, or millions, of would-be workers. The labor union policy of holding off those willing to work would collapse. Market wage rates would prevail once again. It is here that unemployment relief is brought into play and its role [in keeping workers from competing on the labor market] needs no further explanation.

Thus, we see that unemployment, as a long-term mass phenomenon, is the consequence of the labor union policy of driving wage rates up. Without unemployment relief, this policy would have collapsed long ago. Thus, unemployment relief is not a means for alleviating the want caused by unemployment, as is assumed by misguided public opinion. It is, on the contrary, one link in the chain of causes which actually makes unemployment a long-term mass phenomenon.

4.   The Remedy for Mass Unemployment

Appreciation of this relationship has certainly become more widespread in recent years. With all due caution and with a thousand reservations, it is even generally admitted that labor union wage policy is responsible for the extent and duration of unemployment. All serious proposals for fighting unemployment depend on recognition of this theory. When proposals are made to reimburse entrepreneurs, directly or indirectly from public funds, for a part of their wage costs, if they seek to recruit the unemployed in their plants, then it is being recognized that entrepreneurs would employ more workers at a lower wage scale. If it is suggested that the national or municipal government undertake projects without considering their profitability, projects which private enterprise does not want to carry out because they are not profitable, this too simply means that wage rates are so high that they do not permit these undertakings to make profits. (Incidentally, it may be noted that this latter proposal entirely overlooks the fact that a government can build and invest only if it withdraws the necessary means from the private economy. So putting this proposal into effect must lead to just as much new unemployment on one side as it eliminates on the other.)

Then again, if a reduction in hours of work is considered, this too implies recognition of our thesis. For after all, this proposal seeks to shorten the working hours in such a way that all the unemployed will find work, and so that each individual worker, to the extent that he will have less work than he does today, will be entitled to receive less pay. Obviously this assumes that no more work is to be found at the present rate of pay than is currently being provided. The fact that wage rates are too high to give employment to everyone is also admitted by anyone who asks workers to increase production without raising wage rates. It goes without saying that, wherever hourly wages prevail, this means a reduction in the price of labor. If one assumes a cut in the piece rate, labor would also be cheaper where piece work prevails. Obviously then, the crucial factor is not the absolute height of hourly or daily wage rates, but the wage costs which yield a definite output.

However, the demand to reduce wage rates is now also being made openly. In fact, wage rates have already been substantially lowered in many enterprises. Workers are called upon by the press and government officials to relax some of their wage demands and to make a sacrifice for the sake of the general welfare. To make this bearable, the prospect of price cuts is held out to the workers, and the governments try to secure price reductions by putting pressure on the entrepreneurs.

However, it is not a question of reducing wage rates. This bears repeating with considerable emphasis. The problem is to reestablish freedom in the determination of wage rates. It is true that in the beginning this would lead to a reduction in money wage rates for many groups of workers. How far this drop in wage rates must go to eliminate unemployment as a lasting phenomenon can be shown only by the free determination of wage rates on the labor market. Negotiations between union leaders and business combinations, with or without the cooperation of officials, decisions by arbitrators or similar techniques of interventionism are no substitute. The determination of wage rates must become free once again. The formation of wage rates should be hampered neither by the clubs of striking pickets nor by government's apparatus of force. Only if the determination of wage rates is free will they be able to fulfill their function of bringing demand and supply into balance on the labor market.

5.   The Effects of Government Intervention

The demand that a reduction in prices be tied in with the reduction in wage rates ignores the fact that wage rates appear too high precisely because wage reductions have not accompanied the practically universal reduction in prices. Granted, the prices of many articles could not join the drop in prices as they would on an unhampered market, either because they were protected by special governmental interventions (tariffs, for instance) or because they contained substantial costs in the form of taxes and higher than unhampered market wage rates. The decline in the price of coal was held up in Germany because of the rigidity of wage rates which, in the mining of hard coal, come to 56% of the value of production.[1] The domestic price of iron in Germany can remain above the world market price only because tariff policy permits the creation of a national iron cartel and international agreements among national cartels. Here too, one need ask only that those interferences which thwart the free market formation of prices be

---

1. [This address to German industrialists was given in 1931.—Ed.]

abolished. There is no need to call for a price reduction to be dictated by government, labor unions, public opinion or anyone else.

Against the assertion that unemployment is due to the extreme height of wages, it is entirely wrong to introduce the argument that wages are still higher elsewhere. If workers enjoyed complete freedom to move, there would be a tendency throughout the economic world for wage rates for similar work to be uniform. However, in recent years, the freedom of movement for workers has been considerably reduced, even almost completely abolished. The labor unions ask the government to forbid the migration of workers from abroad lest such immigrants frustrate union policy by underbidding the wage rates demanded by the unions.

If there had been no immigration restrictions, millions of workers would have migrated from Europe to the United States in recent decades. This migration would have reduced the differences between American and European wage rates. By stopping immigration into the United States, wage rates are raised there and lowered in Europe. It is not the hardheartedness of European capitalists but the labor policy of the United States (and of Australia and other foreign countries too) which is responsible for the size of the gap between wage rates here in Europe and overseas. After all, the workers in most European countries follow the same policy of keeping out foreign competitors. They, too, restrict or even prohibit foreign workers from coming into their countries so as to protect in this way the labor union policy of holding up wage rates.

6.   The Process of Progress

A popular doctrine makes "rationalization" responsible for unemployment. As a result of "rationalization," practically universal "rationalization," it is held that those workers who cannot find employment anywhere become surplus.

"Rationalization" is a modern term which has been in use for only a short time. The concept, however, is by no means new. The capitalistic entrepreneur is continually striving to make production and marketing more efficient. There have been times when the course of "rationalization" has been relatively more turbulent than in recent years. "Rationalization" was taking place on a large scale when the blacksmith was

replaced by the steel and rolling mills, handweaving and spinning by
mechanical looms and spindles, the stagecoach by the steam engine —
even though the word "rationalization" was not then known and even
though there were then no officials, advisory boards and commissions
with reports, programs and dogmas such as go along with the technical
revolution today.

Industrial progress has always set workers free. There have always
been shortsighted persons who, fearing that no employment would be
found for the released workers, have tried to stop the progress. Workers
have always resisted technical improvement and writers have always
been found to justify this opposition. Every increase in the productivity
of labor has been carried out in spite of the determined resistance of
governments, "philanthropists," "moralists" and workers. If the theory
which attributes unemployment to "rationalization" were correct, then
ninety-nine out of a hundred workers at the end of the nineteenth century would have been out of work.

Workers released by the introduction of industrial technology find
employment in other positions. The ranks of newly developing branches
of industry are filled with these workers. The additional commodities
available for consumption, which come in the wake of "rationalization," are produced with their labor. Today this process is hampered
by the fact that those workers who are released receive unemployment
relief and so do not consider it necessary to change their occupation
and place of work in order to find employment again. It is not on account of "rationalization," but because the unemployed are relieved of
the necessity of looking around for new work, that unemployment has
become a lasting phenomenon.

B. PRICE DECLINES AND PRICE SUPPORTS

1. The Subsidization of Surpluses

The opposition to market determination of prices is not limited to
wages and interest rates. Once the stand is taken not to permit the
structure of market prices to work its effect on production there is no
reason to stop short of commodity prices.

If the prices of coal, sugar, coffee or rye go down, this means that consumers are asking more urgently for other commodities. As a result of the decline in such prices, some concerns producing these commodities become unprofitable and are forced to reduce production or shut down completely. The capital and labor thus released are then shifted to other branches of the economy in order to produce commodities for which a stronger demand prevails.

However, politics interferes once again. It tries to hinder the adjustment of production to the requirements of consumption—by coming to the aid of the producer who is hurt by price reductions.

In recent years, capitalistic methods of production have been applied more and more extensively to the production of raw materials. As always, wherever capitalism prevails, the result has been an astonishing increase in productivity. Grain, fruit, meat, rubber, wool, cotton, oil, copper, coal, minerals are all much more readily available now than they were before the war [World War I] and in the early postwar years. Yet, it was just a short while ago that governments believed they had to devise ways and means to ease the shortage of raw materials. When, without any help from them, the years of plenty came, they immediately took up the cudgels to prevent this wealth from having its full effect for economic well-being. The Brazilian government wants to prevent the decline in the price of coffee so as to protect plantation owners who operate on poorer soil or with less capital from having to cut down or give up cultivation. The much richer United States government wants to stop the decline in the price of wheat and in many other prices because it wants to relieve the farmer working on poorer soil of the need to adjust or discontinue his enterprise.

Tremendous sums are sacrificed throughout the world in completely hopeless attempts to forestall the effects of the improvements made under capitalistic production. Billions are spent in the fruitless effort to maintain prices and in direct subsidy to those producers who are less capable of competing. Further billions are indirectly used for the same goals, through protective tariffs and similar measures which force consumers to pay higher prices. The aim of all these interventions—which drive prices up so high as to keep in business producers who would otherwise be unable to meet competition—can certainly never be attained. However, all these measures delay the processing industries, which use capital and labor, in adjusting their resources to the new supplies of raw materials produced. Thus the increase in commodities represents primarily an embarrassment and not an improvement in living standards. Instead of becoming a blessing for the consumer, the wealth becomes a burden for him, if he must pay for the government interventions in the form of higher taxes and tariffs.

2.   The Need for Readjustments

The cultivation of wheat in central Europe was jeopardized by the increase in overseas production. Even if European farmers were more efficient, more skilled in modern methods and better supplied with capital, even if the prevailing industrial arrangement was not small and pygmy-sized, wasteful, productivity-hampering enterprises, these farms on less fertile soil with less favorable weather conditions still could not rival the wheat farms of Canada. Central Europe must reduce its cultivation of grain, as it cut down on the breeding of sheep decades ago. The billions which the hopeless struggle against the better soil of America has already cost is money uselessly squandered. The future of central European agriculture does not lie in the cultivation of grain. Denmark and Holland have shown that agriculture can exist in Europe even without the protection of tariffs, subsidies and special privileges. However, the economy of central Europe will depend in the future, to a still greater extent than before, on industry.

By this time, it is easy to understand the paradox of the phenomenon that higher yields in the production of raw materials and foodstuffs cause harm. The interventions of governments and of the privileged groups, which seek to hinder the adjustment of the market to the situation brought about by new circumstances, mean that an abundant harvest brings misfortune to everyone.

In recent decades, in almost all countries of the world, attempts have been made to use high protective tariffs to develop economic self-sufficiency (autarky) among smaller and middle-sized domains. Tremendous sums have been invested in manufacturing plants for which there was no economic demand. The result is that we are rich today in physical structures, the facilities of which cannot be fully exploited or perhaps not even used at all.

The result of all these efforts to annul the laws which the market decrees for the capitalistic economy is, briefly, lasting unemployment of many millions, unprofitability for industry and agriculture, and idle factories. As a result of all these, political controversies become seriously aggravated, not only within countries but also among nations.

C. TAX POLICY

1.   The Anti-capitalistic Mentality

The harmful influence of politics on the economy goes far beyond the consequences of the interventionist measures previously discussed.

There is no need to mention the mobilization policies of the government, the continual controversies constantly emerging from nationalistic conflicts in multi-lingual communities and the anxiety caused by saber rattling ministers and political parties. All of these things create unrest. Thus, they may *indirectly* aggravate the crisis situation and especially the uneasiness of the business world.

Financial policy, however, works *directly*.

The share of the people's income which government exacts for its expenditures, even entirely apart from military spending, is continually rising. There is hardly a single country in Europe in which tremendous sums are not being wasted on largely misguided national and municipal economic undertakings. Everywhere, we see government continually taking over new tasks when it is hardly able to carry out satisfactorily its previous obligations. Everywhere, we see the bureaucracy swell in size. As a result, taxes are rising everywhere. At a time when the need to reduce production costs is being universally discussed, new taxes are being imposed on production. Thus the economic crisis is, at the same time, a crisis in public finance also. This crisis in public finance will not be resolved without a complete revision of government operations.

One widely held view, which easily dominates public opinion today, maintains that taxes on wealth are harmless. Thus every governmental expenditure is justified, if the funds to pay for it are not raised by taxing mass consumption or imposing income taxes on the masses. This idea, which must be held responsible for the mania toward extravagance in government expenditures, has caused those in charge of government financial policy to lose completely any feeling of a need for economy.

Spending a large part of the people's income in senseless ways—in order to carry out futile price support operations, to undertake the hopeless task of trying to support with subsidies unprofitable enterprises which could not otherwise survive, to cover the losses of unprofitable public enterprises and to finance the unemployment of millions—would not be justified, even if the funds for the purpose were collected in ways that do not aggravate the crisis. However, tax policy is aimed primarily, or even exclusively, at taxing the yield on capital and the capital itself. This leads to a slowing down of capital formation and even, in many countries, to capital consumption. However, this concerns not capitalists only, as generally assumed. The quantitatively lower the ratio of capital to workers, the lower the wage rates which develop on the free labor market. Thus, even workers are affected by this policy.

Because of tax legislation, entrepreneurs must frequently operate their businesses differently from the way reason would otherwise indicate. As a result, productivity declines and consequently so does the provision of goods for consumption. As might be expected, capitalists shy away from leaving capital in countries with the highest taxation and turn to lands where taxes are lower. It becomes more difficult, on that account, for the system of production to adjust to the changing pattern of economic demand.

Financial policy certainly did not create the crisis. However, it does contribute substantially to making it worse.

D. GOLD PRODUCTION

1.   The Decline in Prices

One popular doctrine blames the crisis on the insufficiency of gold production.

The basic error in this attempt to explain the crisis rests on equating a drop in prices with a crisis. A slow, steady, downward slide in the prices of all goods and services could be explained by the relationship to the production of gold. Businessmen have become accustomed to a relationship of the demand for, and supply of, gold from which a slow steady rise in prices emerges as a secular (continuing) trend. However, they could just as easily have become reconciled to some other arrangement—and they certainly would have if developments had made that necessary. After all, the businessman's most important characteristic is flexibility. The businessman can operate at a profit, even if the general tendency of prices is downward, and economic conditions can even improve then too.

The turbulent price declines since 1929 were definitely not generated by the gold production situation. Moreover, gold production has nothing to do with the fact that the decline in prices is not universal, nor that it does not specifically involve wages also.

It is true that there is a close connection between the quantity of gold produced and the formation of prices. Fortunately, this is no longer in dispute. If gold production had been considerably greater than it actually was in recent years, then the drop in prices would have been moderated or perhaps even prevented from appearing. It would be wrong, however, to assume that the phenomenon of the crisis would not then have occurred. The attempts of labor unions to drive wages up higher than they would have been on the unhampered market and the efforts of governments to alleviate the difficulties of various groups of producers have nothing to do with whether actual money prices are higher or lower.

Labor unions no longer contend over the height of *money* wages, but over the height of *real* wages. It is not because of low prices that producers of rye, wheat, coffee and so on are impelled to ask for government interventions. It is because of the unprofitability of their enterprises. However, the profitability of these enterprises would be no greater, even if prices were higher. For if the gold supply had been increased, not only would the prices of the products which the enterprises in question produce and want to sell have become or have remained proportionately higher, but so also would the prices of all the goods which comprise their costs. Then too, as in any inflation, an increase in the gold supply does not affect all prices at the same time, nor to the same extent. It helps some groups in the economy and hurts others. Thus no reason remains for assuming that an increase in the gold supply must, in a particular case, improve the situation for precisely those producers who now have cause to complain about the unprofitability of their undertakings. It could be that their situation would not only *not* be improved; it might even be worsened.

The error in equating the drop in prices with the crisis and, thus, considering the cause of this crisis to be the insufficient production of gold is especially dangerous. It leads to the view that the crisis could be overcome by increasing the fiduciary media in circulation. Thus the banks are asked to stimulate business conditions with the issue of additional banknotes and an additional credit expansion through credit entries. At first, to be sure, a boom can be generated in this way. However, as we have seen, such an upswing must eventually lead to a collapse in the business outlook and a new crisis.

2.   Inflation as a "Remedy"

It is astonishing that sincere persons can either make such a demand or lend it support. Every possible argument in favor of such a scheme has already been raised a hundred times, and demolished a thousand times over. Only *one* argument is new, although on that account no less false. This is to the effect that the higher than unhampered market wage rates can be brought into proper relationship most easily by an inflation.

This argument shows how seriously concerned our political economists are to avoid displeasing the labor unions. Although they cannot help but recognize that wage rates are too high and must be reduced, they dare not openly call for a halt to such overpayments. Instead, they propose to outsmart the unions in some way. They propose that the actual money wage rate remain unchanged in the coming inflation. In effect, this would amount to reducing the real wage. This assumes, of course, that the unions will refrain from making further wage demands in the ensuing boom and that they will, instead, remain passive while their real wage rates deteriorate. Even if this entirely unjustified optimistic expectation is accepted as true, nothing is gained thereby. A boom caused by banking policy measures must still lead eventually to a crisis and a depression. So, by this method, the problem of lowering wage rates is not resolved but simply postponed.

Yet, all things considered, many may think it advantageous to delay the unavoidable showdown with labor union policy. However, this ignores the fact that, with each artificial boom, large sums of capital are malinvested and, as a result, wasted. Every diminution in society's stock of capital must lead toward a reduction in the "natural" or "static" wage rate. Thus, postponing the decision costs the masses a great deal. Moreover, it will make the final confrontation still more difficult, rather than easier.

IV

Is There a Way Out?

1. The Cause of Our Difficulties

The severe convulsions of the economy are the inevitable result of policies which hamper market activity, the regulator of capitalistic production. If everything possible is done to prevent the market from fulfilling its function of bringing supply and demand into balance, it should come as no surprise that a serious disproportionality between supply and demand persists, that commodities remain unsold, factories stand idle, many millions are unemployed, destitution and misery are growing and that finally, in the wake of all these, destructive radicalism is rampant in politics.

The periodically returning crises of cyclical changes in business conditions are the effect of attempts, undertaken repeatedly, to underbid the interest rates which develop on the unhampered market. These attempts to underbid unhampered market interest rates are made through the intervention of banking policy—by credit expansion through the additional creation of uncovered notes and checking deposits—in order to bring about a boom. The crisis under which we are now suffering is of this type, too. However, it goes beyond the typical business cycle depression, not only in scale but also in character—because the interventions with market processes which evoked the crisis were not limited only to influencing the rate of interest. The interventions have directly affected wage rates and commodity prices, too.

With the economic crisis, the breakdown of interventionist economic policy—the policy being followed today by all governments, irrespective of whether they are responsible to parliaments or rule openly as dictatorships—becomes apparent. This catastrophe obviously comes as no surprise. Economic theory has long been predicting such an outcome to interventionism.

The capitalistic economic system, that is the social system based on private ownership of the means of production, is rejected unanimously today by all political parties and governments. No similar agreement may be found with respect to what economic system should replace it in the future. Many, although not all, look to socialism as the goal. They stubbornly reject the result of the scientific examination of the socialistic ideology, which has demonstrated the unworkability of socialism. They refuse to learn anything from the experiences of the Russian and other European experiments with socialism.

2.   The Unwanted Solution

Concerning the task of present economic policy, however, complete agreement prevails. The goal is an economic arrangement which is assumed to represent a compromise solution, the "middle-of-the-road" between socialism and capitalism. To be sure, there is no intent to abolish private ownership of the means of production. Private property will be permitted to continue, although directed, regulated and controlled by government and by other agents of society's coercive apparatus. With respect to this system of interventionism, the science of economics points out, with incontrovertible logic, that it is contrary to reason; that the interventions which go to make up the system can never accomplish the goals their advocates hope to attain, and that every intervention will have consequences no one wanted.

The capitalistic social order acquires meaning and purpose through the market. Hampering the functions of the market and the formation of prices does not create order. Instead it leads to chaos, to economic crisis.

All attempts to emerge from the crisis by new interventionist measures are completely misguided. There is only *one* way out of the crisis: Forego every attempt to prevent the impact of market prices on production. Give up the pursuit of policies which seek to establish interest rates, wage rates and commodity prices different from those the market indicates. This may contradict the prevailing view. It certainly is not popular. Today all governments and political parties have full confidence in interventionism and it is not likely that they will abandon their program. However, it is perhaps not too optimistic to assume that those governments and parties whose policies have led to this crisis will some day disappear from the stage and make way for men whose economic program leads not to destruction and chaos, but to economic development and progress.

The Current Status of Business Cycle Research and Its Prospects for the Immediate Future

1.   The Acceptance of the Circulation Credit Theory of Business Cycles

It is frequently claimed that if the causes of cyclical changes were understood, economic programs suitable for smoothing out cyclical "waves" would be adopted. The upswing would then be throttled down in time to soften the decline that inevitably follows in its wake. As a result, economic development would proceed at a more even pace. The boom's accompanying side effects, considered by many to be undesirable, would then be substantially, perhaps entirely, eliminated. Most significantly, however, the losses inflicted by the crisis and by the decline, which almost everyone deplores, would be considerably reduced, or even completely avoided.

For many people, this prospect has little appeal. In their opinion, the disadvantages of the depression are not too high a price to pay for the prosperity of the upswing. They say that not everything produced during the boom period is malinvestment, which must be liquidated by the crisis. In their opinion, some of the fruits of the boom remain and the progressing economy cannot do without them. However, most economists have looked on the elimination of cyclical changes as both desirable and necessary. Some came to this position because they thought that, if the economy were spared the shock of recurring crises every few years, it would help to preserve the capitalistic system of which they approved. Others have welcomed the prospect of an age without crises precisely because they saw—in an economy that was not disturbed by business fluctuations—no difficulties in the elimination of the entrepreneurs who, in their view, were merely the superfluous beneficiaries of the efforts of others.

Whether these authors looked on the prospect of smoothing out cyclical waves as favorable or unfavorable, all were of the opinion that a more thorough examination of the cause of periodic economic changes would help produce an age of less severe fluctuations. Were they right?

Economic theory cannot answer this question—it is not a theoretical problem. It is a problem of economic policy or, more precisely, of economic history. Although their measures may produce badly muddled

[Contribution to a Festschrift for Arthur Spiethoff, *Die Stellung und der nächste Zukunft der Konjunkturforschung*, pp. 175–180 (Munich: Duncker & Humblot, 1933). Mises addressed the subject of the Festschrift's title.—Ed.]

results, the persons responsible for directing the course of economic policy are better informed today concerning the consequences of an expansion of circulation credit than were their earlier counterparts, especially those on the European continent. Yet, the question remains. Will measures be introduced again in the future which must lead via a boom to a bust?

The Circulation Credit (Monetary) Theory of the Trade Cycle must be considered the currently prevailing doctrine of cyclical change. Even persons who hold another theory find it necessary to make concessions to the Circulation Credit Theory. Every suggestion made for counteracting the present economic crisis uses reasoning developed by the Circulation Credit Theory. Some insist on rescuing every price from momentary distress, even if such distress comes in the upswing following a new crisis. To do this, they would "prime the pump" by further expanding the quantity of fiduciary media. Others oppose such artificial stimulation, because they want to avoid the illusory credit expansion induced prosperity and the crisis that will inevitably follow.

However, even those who advocate programs to spark and stimulate a boom recognize, if they are not completely hopeless dilettantes and ignoramuses, the conclusiveness of the Circulation Credit Theory's reasoning. They do not contest the truth of the Circulation Credit Theory's objections to their position. Instead, they try to ward them off by pointing out that they propose only a "moderate," a carefully prescribed "dosage" of credit expansion or "monetary creation" which, they say, would merely soften, or bring to a halt, the further decline of prices. Even the term "re-deflation," newly introduced in this connection with such enthusiasm, implies recognition of the Circulation Credit Theory. However, there are also fallacies implied in the use of this term.

2.   The Popularity of Low Interest Rates

The credit expansion which evokes the upswing always originates from the idea that business stagnation must be overcome by "easy money." Attempts to demonstrate that this is *not* the case have been in vain. If anyone argues that lower interest rates have not been constantly portrayed as the ideal goal for economic policy, it can only be due to lack of knowledge concerning economic history and recent economic literature. Practically no one has dared to maintain that it would be desirable to have higher interest rates sooner.[1] People who sought cheap credit clamored for the establishment of credit-issuing banks and for these banks to reduce interest rates. Every measure seized upon to avoid "raising the discount rate" has had its roots in the concept that credit must be made "easy." The fact that reducing interest rates through credit expansion must lead to price increases has generally been ignored. However, the cheap money policy would not have been abandoned even if this *had* been recognized.

Public opinion is not committed to one single view with respect to the height of prices as it is in the case of interest rates. Concerning prices, there have always been two different views: On the one side, the demand of producers for *higher* prices and, on the other side, the demand of consumers for *lower* prices. Governments and political parties have championed both demands, if not at the same time, then shifting from time to time according to the groups of voters whose favors they court at the moment. First one slogan, then another is inscribed on their banners, depending on the temporary shift of prices desired. If prices are going up, they crusade against the rising cost of living. If prices are falling, they profess their desire to do everything possible to assure "reasonable" prices for producers. Still, when it comes to trying to *reduce* prices, they generally sponsor programs which cannot attain that goal. No one wants to adopt the only effective means—the limitation of circulation credit—because they do not want to drive interest rates up.[2] In times of declining prices, however, they have been more than ready to adopt credit expansion measures, as *this* goal is attainable by the means already desired, i.e., by reducing interest rates.

Today, those who would seek to expand circulation credit counter objections by explaining that they only want to adjust for the decline in prices that has already taken place in recent years, or at least to prevent a further decline in prices. Thus, it is claimed, such expansion introduces nothing new. Similar arguments were also heard [during the nineteenth century] at the time of the drive for bimetallism.

1. That has always been so; public opinion has always sided with the debtors. (See Jeremy, Bentham. *Defence of Usury*, 2nd ed., London, 1790, pp. 102ff.) The idea that the creditors are the idle rich, hardhearted exploiters of workers, and that the debtors are the unfortunate poor, has not been abandoned even in this age of bonds, bank deposits and savings accounts.

2. An extreme example: the discount policy of the German Reichsbank in the time of inflation. See Graham, Frank. *Exchange, Prices and Production in Hyper-Inflation Germany, 1920–1923.* Princeton, 1930, pp. 65ff.

3.   The Popularity of Labor Union Policy

It is generally recognized that the social consequences of changes in the value of money—apart from the effect such changes have on the value of monetary obligations—may be attributed solely to the fact that these changes are not effected equally and simultaneously with respect to all goods and services. That is, not all prices rise to the same extent and at the same time. Hardly anyone disputes this today. Moreover, it is no longer denied, as it generally was a few years ago, that the duration of the present crisis is caused primarily by the fact that wage rates and certain prices have become inflexible, as a result of union wage policy and various price support activities. Thus, the rigid wage rates and prices do not fully participate in the downward movement of most prices, or do so only after a protracted delay. In spite of all contradictory political interventions, it is also admitted that the continuing mass unemployment is a necessary consequence of the attempts to maintain wage rates above those that would prevail on the unhampered market. However, in forming economic policy, the correct inference from this is not drawn.

Almost all who propose priming the pump through credit expansion consider it self-evident that money wage rates will not follow the upward movement of prices until their relative excess [over the earlier market prices] has disappeared. Inflationary projects of all kinds are agreed to because no one openly dares to attack the union wage policy, which is approved by public opinion and promoted by government. Therefore, so long as today's prevailing view concerning the maintenance of higher than unhampered market wage rates and the interventionist measures supporting them exists, there is no reason to assume that money wage rates can be held steady in a period of rising prices.

4.   The Effect of Lower than Unhampered Market Interest Rates

The causal connection [between credit expansion and rising prices] is denied still more intensely if the proposal for limiting credit expansion is tied in with certain anticipations. If the entrepreneurs expect low interest rates to continue, they will use the low interest rates as a basis for their computations. Only then will entrepreneurs allow themselves to be tempted, by the offer of more ample and cheaper credit, to consider business enterprises which would not appear profitable at the higher interest rates that would prevail on the unaltered loan market.

If it is publicly proclaimed that care will be taken to stop the creation of additional credit in time, then the hoped-for gains must fail to appear. No entrepreneur will want to embark on a new business if it is clear to him in advance that the business cannot be carried through to completion successfully. The failure of recent pump-priming attempts and statements of the authorities responsible for banking policy make it evident that the time of cheap money will very soon come to an end. If there is talk of restriction in the future, one cannot continue to "prime the pump" with credit expansion.

Economists have long known that every expansion of credit must someday come to an end and that, when the creation of additional credit stops, this stoppage must cause a sudden change in business conditions. A glance at the daily and weekly press in the "boom" years since the middle of the last century shows that this understanding was by no means limited to a few persons. Still the speculators, averse to theory as such, did not know it, and they continued to engage in new enterprises. However, if the governments were to let it be known that the credit expansion would continue only a little longer, then its intention to stop expanding would not be concealed from anyone.

5.　The Questionable Fear of Declining Prices

People today are inclined to *over*value the significance of recent accomplishments in clarifying the business cycle problem and to *under*value the Currency School's tremendous contribution. The benefit which practical cyclical policy could derive from the old Currency School theoreticians has still not been fully exploited. Modern cyclical theory has contributed little to practical policy that could not have been learned from the Currency Theory.

Unfortunately, economic theory is weakest precisely where help is most needed—in analyzing the effects of declining prices. A general decline in prices has always been considered unfortunate. Yet today, even more than ever before, the rigidity of wage rates and the costs of many other factors of production hamper an unbiased consideration of the problem. Therefore, it would certainly be timely now to investigate thoroughly the effects of declining money prices and to analyze the widely held idea that declining prices are incompatible with the increased production of goods and services and an improvement in general welfare. The investigation should include a discussion of whether it is true that only inflationistic steps permit the progressive accumulation of capital and productive facilities. So long as this naive inflationist theory of development is firmly held, proposals for using credit expansion to produce a boom will continue to be successful.

The Currency Theory described some time ago the necessary connection between credit expansion and the cycle of economic changes. Its chain of reasoning was only concerned with a credit expansion limited to one nation. It did not do justice to the situation, of special importance in our age of attempted cooperation among the banks of issue, in which all countries expanded equally. In spite of the Currency Theory's explanation, the banks of issue have persistently advised further expansion of credit.

This strong drive on the part of the banks of issue may be traced back to the prevailing idea that rising prices are useful and absolutely necessary for "progress" and to the belief that credit expansion was a suitable method for keeping interest rates low. The relationship between the issue of fiduciary media and the formation of interest rates is sufficiently explained today, at least for the immediate requirements of determining economic policy. However, what still remains to be explained satisfactorily is the problem of generally declining prices.

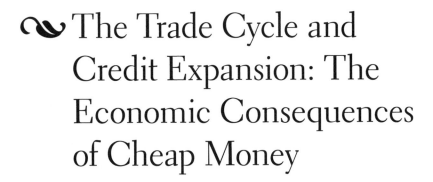 The Trade Cycle and Credit Expansion: The Economic Consequences of Cheap Money

1.   Introductory Remarks

The author of this paper is fully aware of its insufficiency. Yet, there is no means of dealing with the problem of the trade cycle in a more satisfactory way if one does not write a treatise embracing all aspects of the capitalist market economy. The author fully agrees with the dictum of Böhm-Bawerk: "A theory of the trade cycle, if it is not to be mere botching, can only be written as the last chapter or the last chapter but one of a treatise dealing with all economic problems."

It is only with these reservations that the present writer presents this rough sketch to the members of the Committee.

2.   The Unpopularity of Interest

One of the characteristic features of this age of wars and destruction is the general attack launched by all governments and pressure groups against the rights of creditors. The first act of the Bolshevik government was to abolish loans and payment of interest altogether. The most popular of the slogans that swept the Nazis into power was *Brechung der Zinsknechtschaft*, abolition of interest-slavery. The debtor countries are intent upon expropriating the claims of foreign creditors by various devices, the most efficient of which is foreign exchange control. Their economic nationalism aims at brushing away an alleged return to colonialism. They pretend to wage a new war of independence against the foreign exploiters as they venture to call those who provided them with the capital required for the improvement of their economic conditions. As the foremost creditor nation today is the United States, this struggle is virtually directed against the American people. Only the old usages of diplomatic reticence make it advisable for the economic nationalists to name the devil they are fighting not the Yankees, but "Wall Street."

"Wall Street" is no less the target at which the monetary authorities of this country are directing their blows when embarking upon an "easy money" policy. It is generally assumed that measures designed to lower the rate of interest below the height at which the unhampered

[A memorandum, dated April 24, 1946, written in English by Professor Mises to a committee of businessmen.—Ed.]

market would fix it are extremely beneficial to the immense majority at the expense of a small minority of capitalists and hardboiled money-lenders. It is tacitly implied that the creditors are the idle rich while the debtors are the industrious poor. However, this belief is atavistic and utterly misjudges contemporary conditions.

In the days of Solon, Athens' wise legislator, in the time of ancient Rome's agrarian laws, in the Middle Ages and even for some centuries later, one was by and large right in identifying the creditors with the rich and the debtors with the poor. It is quite different in our age of bonds and debentures, of savings banks, of life insurance and social security. The proprietory classes are the owners of big plants and farms, of common stock, of urban real estate and, as such, they are very often debtors. The people of more modest income are bondholders, own-ers of saving deposits and insurance policies and beneficiaries of social security. As such, they are creditors. Their interests are impaired by endeavors to lower the rate of interest and the national currency's pur-chasing power.

It is true that the masses do not think of themselves as creditors and thus sympathize with the anti-creditor policies. However, this igno-rance does not alter the fact that the immense majority of the nation are to be classified as creditors and that these people, in approving of an "easy money" policy, unwittingly hurt their own material interests. It merely explodes the Marxian fable that a social class never errs in recognizing its particular class interests and always acts in accordance with these interests.

The modern champions of the "easy money" policy take pride in calling themselves unorthodox and slander their adversaries as ortho-dox, old-fashioned and reactionary. One of the most eloquent spokes-men of what is called functional finance, Professor Abba Lerner, pre-tends that in judging fiscal measures he and his friends resort to what "is known as the method of science as opposed to scholasticism." The truth is that Lord Keynes, Professor Alvin H. Hansen and Professor Lerner, in their passionate denunciation of interest, are guided by the essence of Medieval Scholasticism's economic doctrine, the disappro-bation of interest. While emphatically asserting that a return to the nineteenth century's economic policies is out of the question, they are zealously advocating a revival of the methods of the Dark Ages and of the orthodoxy of old canons.

3.   The Two Classes of Credit

There is no difference between the ultimate objectives of the anti-interest policies of canon law and the policies recommended by modern interest-baiting. But the methods applied are different. Medieval orthodoxy was intent first upon prohibiting by decree interest altogether and later upon limiting the height of interest rates by the so-called usury laws. Modern self-styled unorthodoxy aims at lowering or even abolishing interest by means of credit expansion.

Every serious discussion of the problem of credit expansion must start from the distinction between two classes of credit: commodity credit and circulation credit.

Commodity credit is the transfer of savings from the hands of the original saver into those of the entrepreneurs who plan to use these funds in production. The original saver has saved money by not consuming what he could have consumed by spending it for consumption. He transfers purchasing power to the debtor and thus enables the latter to buy these non-consumed commodities for use in further production. Thus the amount of commodity credit is strictly limited by the amount of saving, i.e., abstention from consumption. Additional credit can only be granted to the extent that additional savings have been accumulated. The whole process does not affect the purchasing power of the monetary unit.

Circulation credit is credit granted out of funds especially created for this purpose by the banks. In order to grant a loan, the bank prints banknotes or credits the debtor on a deposit account. It is creation of credit out of nothing. It is tantamount to the creation of fiat money, to undisguised, manifest inflation. It increases the amount of money substitutes, of things which are taken and spent by the public in the same way in which they deal with money proper. It increases the buying power of the debtors. The debtors enter the market of factors of production with an additional demand, which would not have existed except for the creation of such banknotes and deposits. This additional demand brings about a general tendency toward a rise in commodity prices and wage rates.

While the quantity of commodity credit is rigidly fixed by the amount of capital accumulated by previous saving, the quantity of circulation credit depends on the conduct of the bank's business. Commodity credit cannot be expanded, but circulation credit can. Where there is no circulation credit, a bank can only increase its lending to the extent that the savers have entrusted it with more deposits. Where there is circulation credit, a bank can expand its lending by what is, curiously enough, called "being more liberal."

Credit expansion not only brings about an inextricable tendency for commodity prices and wage rates to rise. It also affects the market rate of interest. As it represents an additional quantity of money offered for loans, it generates a tendency for interest rates to drop below the height they would have reached on a loan market not manipulated by credit expansion. It owes its popularity with quacks and cranks not only to the inflationary rise in prices and wage rates which it engenders, but no less to its short-run effect of lowering interest rates. It is today the main tool of policies aiming at cheap or easy money.

4.   The Function of Prices, Wage Rates and Interest Rates

The rate of interest is a market phenomenon. In the market economy it is the structure of prices, wage rates and interest rates, as determined by the market, that directs the activities of the entrepreneurs toward those lines in which they satisfy the wants of the consumers in the best possible and cheapest way. The prices of the material factors of production, wage rates and interest rates on the one hand and the anticipated future prices of the consumers' goods on the other hand are the items that enter into the planning businessman's calculations. The result of these calculations shows the businessman whether or not a definite project will pay. If the market data underlying his calculations are falsified by the interference of the government, the result must be misleading. Deluded by an arithmetical operation with illusory figures, the entrepreneurs embark upon the realization of projects that are at variance with the most urgent desires of consumers. The disagreement of the consumers becomes manifest when the products of capital malinvestment reach the market and cannot be sold at satisfactory prices. Then, there appears what is called "bad business."

If, on a market not hampered by government tampering with the market data, the examination of a definite project shows its unprofitability, it is proved that under the given state of affairs the consumers prefer the execution of other projects. The fact that a definite business venture is not profitable means that the consumers, in buying its products, are not ready to reimburse entrepreneurs for the prices of the complementary factors of production required, while on the other hand, in buying other products, they are ready to reimburse entrepreneurs for the prices of the same factors. Thus the sovereign consumers express their wishes and force business to adjust its activities to the satisfaction of those wants which they consider the most urgent. The consumers thus bring about a tendency for profitable industries to expand and for unprofitable ones to shrink.

It is permissible to say that what proximately prevents the execution of certain projects is the state of prices, wage rates and interest rates. It is a serious blunder to believe that if only these items were lower, production activities could be expanded. What limits the size of production is the scarcity of the factors of production. Prices, wage rates and interest rates are only indices expressive of the degree of this scarcity. They are pointers, as it were. Through these market phenomena, society sends out a warning to the entrepreneurs planning a definite project: Don't touch this factor of production; it is earmarked for the satisfaction of another, more urgent need.

The expansionists, as the champions of inflation style themselves today, see in the rate of interest nothing but an obstacle to the expansion of production. If they were consistent, they would have to look in the same way at the prices of the material factors of production and at wage rates. A government decree cutting down wage rates to 50% of those on the unhampered labor market would likewise give to certain projects, which do not appear profitable in a calculation based on the actual market data, the appearance of profitability. There is no more sense in the assertion that the height of interest rates prevents a further expansion of production than in the assertion that the height of wage rates brings about these effects. The fact that the expansionists apply this kind of fallacious argumentation only to interest rates and not also to the prices of primary commodities and to the prices of labor is the proof that they are guided by emotions and passions and not by cool reasoning. They are driven by resentment. They envy what they believe is the rich man's take. They are unaware of the fact that in attacking interest they are attacking the broad masses of savers, bondholders and beneficiaries of insurance policies.

5.   The Effects of Politically Lowered Interest Rates

The expansionists are quite right in asserting that credit expansion succeeds in bringing about booming business. They are mistaken only in ignoring the fact that such an artificial prosperity cannot last and must inextricably lead to a slump, a general depression.

If the market rate of interest is reduced by credit expansion, many projects which were previously deemed unprofitable get the appearance of profitability. The entrepreneur who embarks upon their execution must, however, very soon discover that his calculation was based on erroneous assumptions. He has reckoned with those prices of the factors of production which corresponded to market conditions as they were on the eve of the credit expansion. But now, as a result of credit expansion, these prices have risen. The project no longer appears so promising as before. The businessman's funds are not sufficient for the purchase of the required factors of production. He would be forced to discontinue the pursuit of his plans if the credit expansion were not to continue. However, as the banks do not stop expanding credit and providing business with "easy money," the entrepreneurs see no cause to worry. They borrow more and more. Prices and wage rates boom. Everybody feels happy and is convinced that now finally mankind has overcome forever the gloomy state of scarcity and reached everlasting prosperity.

In fact, all this amazing wealth is fragile, a castle built on the sands of illusion. It cannot last. There is no means to substitute banknotes and deposits for non-existing capital goods. Lord Keynes, in a poetical mood, asserted that credit expansion has performed "the miracle . . . of turning a stone into bread."[1] But this miracle, on closer examination, appears no less questionable than the tricks of Indian fakirs.

There are only two alternatives.

One, the expanding banks may stubbornly cling to their expansionist policies and never stop providing the money business needs in order to go on in spite of the inflationary rise in production costs. They are intent upon satisfying the ever increasing demand for credit. The more credit business demands, the more it gets. Prices and wage rates sky-rocket. The quantity of banknotes and deposits increases beyond all

---

1. *Paper of the British Experts*, April 8, 1943.

measure. Finally, the public becomes aware of what is happening. People realize that there will be no end to the issue of more and more money substitutes—that prices will consequently rise at an accelerated pace. They comprehend that under such a state of affairs it is detrimental to keep cash. In order to prevent being victimized by the progressing drop in money's purchasing power, they rush to buy commodities, no matter what their prices may be and whether or not they need them. They prefer everything else to money. They arrange what in 1923 in Germany, when the Reich set the classical example for the policy of endless credit expansion, was called *die Flucht in die Sachwerte,* the flight into real values. The whole currency system breaks down. Its unit's purchasing power dwindles to zero. People resort to barter or to the use of another type of foreign or domestic money. The crisis emerges.

The other alternative is that the banks or the monetary authorities become aware of the dangers involved in endless credit expansion before the common man does. They stop, of their own accord, any further addition to the quantity of banknotes and deposits. They no longer satisfy the business applications for additional credits. Then the panic breaks out. Interest rates jump to an excessive level, because many firms badly need money in order to avoid bankruptcy. Prices drop suddenly, as distressed firms try to obtain cash by throwing inventories on the market dirt cheap. Production activities shrink, workers are discharged.

Thus, credit expansion unavoidably results in the economic crisis. In either of the two alternatives, the artificial boom is doomed. In the long run, it must collapse. The short-run effect, the period of prosperity, may last sometimes several years. While it lasts, the authorities, the expanding banks and their public relations agencies arrogantly defy the warnings of the economists and pride themselves on the manifest success of their policies. But when the bitter end comes, they wash their hands of it.

The artificial prosperity cannot last because the lowering of the rate of interest, purely technical as it was and not corresponding to the real state of the market data, has misled entrepreneurial calculations. It has created the illusion that certain projects offer the chances of profitability when, in fact, the available supply of factors of production was not sufficient for their execution. Deluded by false reckoning, businessmen have expanded their activities beyond the limits drawn by the state of society's wealth. They have underrated the degree of the scarcity of factors of production and overtaxed their capacity to produce. In short: they have squandered scarce capital goods by malinvestment.

The whole entrepreneurial class is, as it were, in the position of a master builder whose task it is to construct a building out of a limited supply of building materials. If this man overestimates the quantity of the available supply, he drafts a plan for the execution of which the means at his disposal are not sufficient. He overbuilds the groundwork and the foundations and discovers only later, in the progress of the construction, that he lacks the material needed for the completion of the structure. This belated discovery does not create our master builder's plight. It merely discloses errors committed in the past. It brushes away illusions and forces him to face stark reality.

There is need to stress this point, because the public, always in search of a scapegoat, is as a rule ready to blame the monetary authorities and the banks for the outbreak of the crisis. They are guilty, it is asserted, because in stopping the further expansion of credit, they have produced a deflationary pressure on trade. Now, the monetary authorities and the banks were certainly responsible for the orgies of credit expansion and the resulting boom; although public opinion, which always approves such inflationary ventures wholeheartedly, should not forget that the fault rests not alone with others. The crisis is not an outgrowth of the abandonment of the expansionist policy. It is the inextricable and unavoidable aftermath of this policy. The question is only whether one should continue expansionism until the final collapse of the whole monetary and credit system or whether one should stop at an earlier date. The sooner one stops, the less grievous are the damages inflicted and the losses suffered.

Public opinion is utterly wrong in its appraisal of the phases of the trade cycle. The artificial boom is not prosperity, but the deceptive appearance of good business. Its illusions lead people astray and cause malinvestment and the consumption of unreal apparent gains which amount to virtual consumption of capital. The depression is the necessary process of readjusting the structure of business activities to the real state of the market data, i.e., the supply of capital goods and the valuations of the public. The depression is thus the first step on the return to normal conditions, the beginning of recovery and the foundation of real prosperity based on the solid production of goods and not on the sands of credit expansion.

Additional credit is sound in the market economy only to the extent that it is evoked by an increase in the public's savings and the resulting increase in the amount of commodity credit. Then, it is the public's conduct that provides the means needed for additional investment. If the public does not provide these means, they cannot be conjured up by the magic of banking tricks. The rate of interest, as it is determined on a loan market not manipulated by an "easy money" policy, is expressive of the people's readiness to withhold from current consumption a part of the income really earned and to devote it to a further expansion of business. It provides the businessman reliable guidance in determining how far he may go in expanding investment, what projects are in compliance with the true size of saving and capital accumulation and what are not. The policy of artificially lowering the rate of interest below its potential market height seduces the entrepreneurs to embark upon certain projects of which the public does not approve. In the market economy, each member of society has his share in determining the amount of additional investment. There is no means of fooling the public all of the time by tampering with the rate of interest. Sooner or later, the public's disapproval of a policy of over-expansion takes effect. Then the airy structure of the artificial prosperity collapses.

Interest is not a product of the machinations of rugged exploiters. The discount of future goods as against present goods is an eternal category of human action and cannot be abolished by bureaucratic measures. As long as there are people who prefer one apple available today to two apples available in twenty-five years, there will be interest. It does not matter whether society is organized on the basis of private ownership of the means of production, viz., capitalism, or on the basis of public ownership, viz., socialism or communism. For the conduct of affairs by a totalitarian government, interest, the different valuation of present and of future goods, plays the same role it plays under capitalism.

Of course, in a socialist economy, the people are deprived of any means to make their own value judgments prevail and only the government's value judgments count. A dictator does not bother whether or not the masses approve of his decision of how much to devote for current consumption and how much for additional investment. If the dictator invests more and thus curtails the means available for current consumption, the people must eat less and hold their tongues. No crisis emerges, because the subjects have no opportunity to utter their dissatisfaction. But in the market economy, with its economic democracy, the consumers are supreme. Their buying or abstention from buying creates entrepreneurial profit or loss. It is the ultimate yardstick of business activities.

6.   The Inevitable Ending

It is essential to realize that what makes the economic crisis emerge is the public's disapproval of the expansionist ventures made possible by the manipulation of the rate of interest. The collapse of the house of cards is a manifestation of the democratic process of the market.

It is vain to object that the public favors the policy of cheap money. The masses are misled by the assertions of the pseudo-experts that cheap money can make them prosperous at no expense whatever. They do not realize that investment can be expanded only to the extent that more capital is accumulated by savings. They are deceived by the fairy tales of monetary cranks from John Law down to Major C. H. Douglas. Yet, what counts in reality is not fairy tales, but people's conduct. If men are not prepared to save more by cutting down their current consumption, the means for a substantial expansion of investment are lacking. These means cannot be provided by printing banknotes or by loans on the bank books.

In discussing the situation as it developed under the expansionist pressure on trade created by years of cheap interest rates policy, one must be fully aware of the fact that the termination of this policy will make visible the havoc it has spread. The incorrigible inflationists will cry out against alleged deflation and will advertise again their patent medicine, inflation, rebaptising it re-deflation. What generates the evils is the expansionist policy. Its termination only makes the evils visible. This termination must at any rate come sooner or later, and the later it comes, the more severe are the damages which the artificial boom has caused. As things are now, after a long period of artificially low interest rates, the question is not how to avoid the hardships of the process of recovery altogether, but how to reduce them to a minimum. If one does not terminate the expansionist policy in time by a return to balanced budgets, by abstaining from government borrowing from the commercial banks and by letting the market determine the height of interest rates, one chooses the German way of 1923.

INDEX

agriculture, 164–65, 171, 172
American colonies, 12–13, 23
anarchy myth, capitalism's production
   activity, 155–56
Austria, post–World War I inflation, 8n3

balance of payments doctrine, 26–28,
   46–50
banking legislation, 125–26, 149. *See also*
   interest rates; interventionist policy
Banking School doctrine, 67, 105–7, 122,
   130
barter, xiii–xiv
Bastiat, Frédéric, 132
Böhm-Bawerk, Eugen von, 55, 189
boom stage, 130, 141–42, 161–62, 194–96.
   See also circulation credit theory;
   interest rates
borrowing effects, reparation payments,
   35–38
Brazil, coffee production, 171
business cycle research: expectations for
   policy, 181–82; forecasting potential,
   145–47; theory evolution, 53–56,
   99–104, 131–32. *See also* circulation
   credit theory

cash and purchase panics, 5–6, 8–9, 195
Chartism, 21
circulation credit theory: overview,
   102–7, 160–61; acceptance of, 102–3,
   182; and business cycle regularity,
   103–4, 117–24; as foundation of cyclical policy, 131–32, 137–38, 152; and

Harvard Barometer, 134–35; interest
   rate patterns, 106–11, 113–14; investment patterns, 112–16, 126–27, 184–85
commodity credit, 191–92, 197
commodity prices. *See* prices
consumer role, in free market operation,
   156–59, 192–93
credit transactions. *See* interest rates
Currency Theory, 100, 109, 128–29,
   131–32, 148–49, 185–86. *See also* circulation credit theory
cyclical policy, 131–38, 148–52

debtors, public opinion, 90, 183n1,
   189–90. *See also* interest rates
demand for money: and foreign trade,
   48–49; and gold prices, 62–64; inflation effects, 5–11; and purchase panics, 5–6, 8–9, 195
demonetization process, 6
depreciation of money: chronology,
   17–18; and devaluation, 23–25; as ideology problem, 43–44; from inflation,
   5–11; reform requirement, 15–16; and
   reparation payment methods, 36–37.
   See also inflation
devaluation, 23–25

economic theory. *See* business cycle
   research; circulation credit theory
entrepreneurs. *See* production activity
exchange rates, 22–30, 45–50, 150–51. *See
   also* foreign money
exports/imports. *See* foreign trade

The typeface used in setting this book is Electra, designed in 1935 by the great American typographer William Addison Dwiggins. Dwiggins was a student and associate of Frederic Goudy and served for a time as acting director of Harvard University Press. In his illustrious career as typographer and book designer (he coined the term "graphic designer"), Dwiggins created a number of typefaces, including Metro and Caledonia, and designed many of the typographic ornaments, or "dingbats," familiar to readers.

Electra is a crisp, elegant, and readable typeface, strongly suggestive of calligraphy. The contrast between its strokes is relatively muted, and it produces an even but still "active" impression in text. Interestingly, the design of the *italic* form—called "cursive" in this typeface—is less calligraphic than the italic form of many faces and more closely resembles the roman.

This book is printed on paper that is acid-free and meets the requirements of the American National Standard for Permanence of Paper for Printed Library Materials, z39.48–1992. ♾

Book design adapted by Erin Kirk New, Watkinsville, Georgia, after a design by Martin Lubin Graphic Design, Jackson Heights, New York

Typography by Newgen, Austin, Texas

Printed and bound by Sheridan Books, Inc., Ann Arbor, Michigan